OPENING THE MIND'S EYE

Christopher Zielinski
144 Sagebrush Street
Oshawa, ON
L1J 7X3

green
press
INITIATIVE

OPENING THE MIND'S EYE

Clarity and Spaciousness in Buddhist Practice

Venerable Master Hsing Yun

TRANSLATED BY AMY LAM

Lantern Books • New York

A Division of Booklight Inc.

2005
Lantern Books
One Union Square West, Suite 201
New York, NY 10003

Printed in Canada

Library of Congress Cataloging-in-Publication Data

Xingyun, da shi.
  Opening the mind's eye : clarity and spaciousness in Buddhist practice / Hsing Yun ; translated by Amy Lam.
    p. cm.
  ISBN 1-59056-093-0 (alk. paper)
  1. Buddhism—Doctrines. 2. Fo Guang Shan Buddhist Order—Doctrines. I. Lam, Amy. II. Title.
BQ9800.F6392X5546 2005
294.3'444—dc22
                                        2005018593

TABLE OF CONTENTS

PREFACE

Many of us view the world through a murky filter, unaware that a glimpse through the lens of the Dharma removes the cloudiness, leaving only brilliance, clarity, and indescribable joy. Venerable Master Hsing Yun has dedicated his life to helping innumerable people put on Dharma glasses and look at their precious lives through new eyes—eyes that see the true nature of the universe and human existence. In this book, Master Hsing Yun expounds upon basic teachings that help us understand conscious and conscientious Buddhist practices and perspectives, enabling us to heighten the value of existence, live a life of utmost freedom and potential, and bring unlimited joy to ourselves and others.

At times we struggle to understand that life can be bigger and more inclusive than our self-imposed boundaries and limitations suggest. We often get stuck in a quagmire of doubt, confusion, animosity, and discontent, creating a life of small dimensions and looming obstacles. A journey through this book can help us examine how we may be perceiving certain aspects of our lives with eyes that are not yet able to manage a more expansive view. Master Hsing Yun shares his insights about spiritually developed ways of thinking and living that can assist us in transcending the plane of ordinary perception.

The themes of dissolving illusive boundaries and penetrating ultimate Truth permeate this entire work. The first chapter builds a foundation upon which the other chapters rely in their quest to unshackle us from our standard, narrow, and even erroneous perspectives. We learn that by embarking on a journey of practice that originates from the "right perspectives," we can open ourselves up to unimpeded spiritual progress that ultimately reveals our true nature. As we nurture deeper awareness and understanding of Buddhist perspectives and delve into new ways of perceiving causes and conditions, time and space, destiny, magic, and rebirth, we can take a first step toward creating a life of immense proportions.

Central to the teachings incorporated in this book and also key to Buddhist thought are the notions of impermanence and the need to rely upon our own efforts to reach ultimate liberation. The reader will encounter numerous references to the importance of understanding the impermanent nature of all phenomena, for this understanding is crucial to gaining freedom from small-mindedness and perpetual suffering. Without realizing the truth of impermanence, we tend to approach life with grasping and clinging attitudes, and therefore may experience continual dissatisfaction and loss. Thus traditional and habitual perceptions keep us mired in suffering. With a mindful and reflective journey through this book, we can begin to understand impermanence in a new way, and see that it points directly to the Dharma, which is both eternal and unchanging.

To facilitate this understanding, Master Hsing Yun elaborates on myriad ways in which we cling to conclusions about own circumstances, traditional ideas about the size and scope of space and time, incorrect assumptions about our own destinies, blindness about magic in daily living, and misunderstandings about rebirth. Although raised in traditional Chinese monasteries, Master Hsing Yun has a keen sense of the daily challenges of modern life, rendering him sensitive to the difficulties we face when attempting to "let go." With the help of this book, we can discover the truth of impermanence, and our lives can blossom with unlimited hope and infinite possibilities. Suddenly, the world is a much more dynamic and creative place.

Woven throughout the pages of this book is the assertion that, quite simply, "it is up to you." Self-effort and self-reliance are essential to enlarging our viewpoints, shifting our perspectives, and finding freedom and joy within Buddhist teachings. Realizing the vast potential and radiant purity inherent in our true nature takes courage and commitment, but the rewards are infinite and exquisite. Along with reasons and specific methods for incorporating the teachings into our daily lives, Master Hsing Yun also offers abundant encouragement for people wanting to venture into the bright world of Buddhist perspectives and practice. While the notion that "it is up to you" may be unsettling or even daunting to those raised in other spiritual traditions, no one needs to be alarmed at this prospect or feel that they are alone or without support. In fact, through practice, we can tap into the beauty of interdependence and realize the harmony and inherent connections between all beings. We will be supported and cradled by the Dharma as we learn to support it in every thought, word, and action.

The numerous affirmations in the first chapter will comfort us, and although learning, studying, practicing, and contemplating elevate and expand our spiritual development, we do not need to acquire anything new or attain copious knowledge in order to fully comprehend the meaning of Buddhist teachings, and ultimately, the Truth. We already possess the Truth; in fact, we *are* the Truth. We only need to wake up and reveal its magnificence. In actuality, this book does not give us anything that we do not already know; our pure, essential Buddha Nature already encompasses complete and perfect understanding. This book will, however, give us tools with which to access this true nature, realize its infinite dimensions, and manifest its perfection and beauty in every moment. We discover that each precious moment of our lives has the potential to enshroud us in confusion, distress, and an atrophied mind, or to invite us into peace, joy, and boundless freedom.

Through the wisdom shared within the pages of this book and the hopeful shift in perception that can occur, Master Hsing Yun invites us to find ease in every moment and "face life and the future with confidence and radiance." Dissolving illusive boundaries and penetrating ultimate Truth are not beyond our comprehension or ability. May you experience abundant joy as you put on your Dharma glasses and experience the true potential and immensity of your life.

BRENDA BOLINGER

CHAPTER ONE

PERCEPTION AND UNDERSTANDING

We all have different ways of looking at things, from the way we look at the nature of existence to the way we perceive the vast universe. As our vantage points are different, our perspectives also vary. Unfortunately, not all of our perspectives are viewed through the lens of the Dharma. Because our original nature, or Buddha Nature, has been clouded repeatedly by worldly distractions and mental confusion, we no longer perceive the world with clarity, and a misguided understanding inevitably results. How do we nurture the right perception and understanding to see life as it truly is? This is the important question that we will address through examining different types and origins of erroneous views, various levels of perception and understanding, and Buddhist teachings that enable the right perspective.

Twenty five hundred years ago, the Buddha, sitting on a "diamond throne" under a bodhi tree, awakened to the true nature of the universe and human existence. After his enlightenment, his first thought was to share his realization of truth with all beings. The truth to which he awakened, however, is contrary to the harmful, misguided way of understanding and perspectives that most people uphold.

For instance, while most people regard the *five desires* (wealth, beauty, fame, food, and sleep) as sources of pleasure, the Buddha considers them to be the root of suffering. Whereas the Buddha sees the Buddha Nature that all beings share as the true reality of existence and the home of ultimate freedom and bliss, most of us find that illusive and unreal. Even though we sentient beings rise and fall aimlessly in the cycle of suffering as we move from one existence to another on the wheel of rebirth, we continue to refuse the compassionate deliverance the Buddha extends to us.

When the Enlightened One contemplated how difficult it would be for sentient beings to accept the truth he had realized, he considered the idea of immediately entering the peaceful state of nirvana, in order to inspire their faith in the Dharma. However, the heavenly devas begged the Bhagavat to remain engaged in this world, and out of compassion, he decided to stay in order to teach the Dharma. Yet, despite all his teachings—that we already possess truth and only need to wake up to its presence—we have such stubborn and habitual attachments to erroneous views that we often confront tremendous difficulties in clarifying our minds.

At times, we encounter people who have different perspectives from us, and senseless arguments ensue due to our limited thinking. For example, monastic life is often pitied and we receive comments such as, "Oh! How regrettable that you chose to renounce the world!" Renunciation is a path of pursuing the truth of life and the universe. It is something to be celebrated. In a life dedicated to understanding the nature of reality and eliminating suffering for all beings, how can there be any regrets? Thus, when we look at the world, we should try to see it not just from our own limited point of view but also from the perspective of others. In this way, we can maintain objectivity and increase our understanding and acceptance of others.

Many people approach religion with little faith and reverence. To them, religion is a means to accumulate wealth and avoid misfortune; it is a tool for acquiring fame and fortune. The joy that comes from understanding that the true meaning of religion lies in giving remains hidden to them.

Once, a devotee complained to me, "Master, I don't want to recite the name of the Buddha anymore."

"Why not?" I questioned. "You have been faithfully chanting the name of the Buddha for over twenty years. Why stop now?"

The devotee replied indignantly, "I thought that chanting the name of the Buddha would bring me good luck in business. Recently, I invested in a business with my friends, but they embezzled my money, leaving me destitute. The Buddha and bodhisattvas did not protect me. Why should I continue to chant the Buddha's name?"

Upon hearing his reply, I suddenly realized that he viewed the Buddha as a deity of wealth, and paying homage to the Buddha was an insurance policy for his finances. How can someone with such a narrow and greedy attitude remain open to the great compassion of the Buddhas and bodhisattvas?

Another devotee once complained to me, "Master! I don't want to be a vegetarian anymore. Although I have been a vegetarian for decades, I still have poor health and am in constant need of medical attention."

When one becomes a vegetarian not out of compassion for all sentient beings, but solely as a means for achieving good health and longevity, the attitude is flawed and the practice remains hollow. Good health comes from disciplined living, good diet, and regular exercise. Like the Buddha, we should practice vegetarianism out of compassion for all sentient beings. This correct perception and attitude will not only help our mental health, but over time can also improve our physical health. Thus correct views can help us avoid traps of folly, while clouded and incorrect views lead only to faulty expectations and stagnant practice. What do the Buddhist teachings tell us about perception and understanding? I shall devote the remainder of the chapter to this question.

ERRONEOUS VIEWS

A person who lacks the correct view is like a ship without a rudder, drifting aimlessly in the vast ocean with potentially disastrous consequences. Erroneous views can trap us in delusions, causing us to habitually speak and act out of confusion and misery. It is of utmost importance that we pursue and maintain the right view. First, let us understand the concept of erroneous views. According to the Buddhist sutras, there are five types of erroneous views: delusions about the physical body, biased views, corrupt views, egotistical views, and views that misuse the precepts.

Delusions about the Physical Body

Although the body exists due to the amalgamation of the four great elements (earth, water, fire, and wind) and the five aggregates (form, feeling, perception, mental formation, and consciousness), many people consider it to be real and permanent. They become attached to their physical form and dependent on its existence. They do not understand that the physical body is similar to a house—even the best-built house will eventually fall apart, and its tenant will have to move out. Those who maintain erroneous views regarding the body consider it to be real and are thus relentless in their pursuit of sensory pleasures. Dimensions beyond that of their physical body remain elusive to people burdened by this attached way of thinking.

Biased Views

Biased views are one-sided and look at only one aspect of a phenomenon. For example, some people have an "eternalistic view" and believe that the world is forever here and unchanging. Others have a "nihilistic view" and believe that all ends with the cessation of life. Those with a "limited view" believe that the world is bounded, while those with an "unbounded view" believe that the world has no fixed boundary. Those who hold the "identical view" believe that the body and mind are one, while those who hold the "dissimilar view" believe that the body and mind are separate. Those who take the "existent view" believe that the Buddha still exists after nirvana, while those who take the "non-existent view" believe that the Buddha ceases to exist after nirvana. These views are all one-sided, impartial, and incomplete; thus they are called "biased views." Biased views suggest thinking with a lack of integration, and they carry unfortunate consequences that stem from ignorance.

Nihilists believe that death is final and that a person's deeds, whether good or bad, bear no consequences. In the scope of nihilistic views, morality and ethics have very little value and are relegated below the pursuit of pleasure. Eternalists, on the other hand, believe in the permanent existence of human life and that an unchanging soul will always exist, even beyond death. They do not understand that the circumstances of rebirth are based on our karma.

These biased views, regardless of whether they are eternalistic, nihilistic, limited, unbounded, identical, or dissimilar, all deviate from the Middle Way and are, consequently, erroneous. The Middle Way advocates avoiding all extremes and not adhering to one philosophy to the exclusion of another. Pursuing a deeper understanding of the Middle Way enables people to realize the true nature of life and existence, and therefore to hold a correct view.

Corrupt Views

To have corrupt views is to harbor understandings that are unethical and unwholesome. Examples include disregarding one's parents, being disrespectful of the Triple Gem—the

Buddha, the Dharma and the Sangha—and not acknowledging the truth of cause and effect. Corrupt views can dull our wisdom and obscure the truth. Some people have a misguided understanding of the Law of Cause and Effect. The Law of Cause and Effect tells us that "the planting of melons yields melons, and the sowing of peas begets peas." But some erroneously deduce from this argument that if one kills a mosquito or a fly, then one will be reborn as a mosquito or fly; or, worse, that if one were to take the life of a man, he would be reborn as a man. This type of warped logic distorts the direct relation of cause and effect, completely misrepresenting the truth of this universal Law. In the examples above, the act of killing logically sows the seed of being killed. This is what is meant by the Law of Cause and Effect, and the truth of "you reap what you sow" will never change. Misrepresentation of the truth is like taking pictures without focusing first; the pictures will come out blurred and fuzzy.

As I have mentioned, many people approach religion as a stepping stone to fortune and fame. They believe that gods will bring them success, wealth, and elevated status. They do not understand that religious cultivation and the pursuit of wealth have their respective and distinct conditions, causes and effects. If we do not have a clear understanding of the merit of our intentions and how different causes yield different effects, we will undoubtedly face grave disappointment and be trapped by our self-righteous attitudes.

There once was an ambitious young man whose goal in life was to be successful and wealthy. He heard that a nearby temple honored a very powerful deity who could answer his wish for wealth. Early one morning, he rode his motorcycle to the temple to present an offering and make his wish to the temple god. After he finished, he got on his bike and took off speeding down the highway, enjoying himself until he lost control and smashed into a guardrail. He was killed instantly. When his father heard the news, he rushed to the temple, pointed an accusing finger at the statue of the deity, and began to curse, "My son faithfully made offerings to you. Not only did you deny him great fortune, you failed to protect him, and now he is dead. You are an unresponsive and worthless god! Today, I will tear down your temple brick by brick!"

In a fury, he rolled up his sleeves to strike the statue. Recognizing the dire situation, the caretaker of the temple tried to reason with the father, "Sir! Please don't be upset. Yes, your son came to pay homage to the temple god. The temple god was moved, and through his compassion and devotion, he wanted to save your son. Unfortunately, the motorcycle on which your son zoomed away was just too fast even for the temple god's celestial horse. It is tragic that your son was killed in the collision, but it was not the deity's fault."

The accident was the logical result of the young man's reckless speeding. Even a respectful tribute to a god does not protect us from the Law of Cause and Effect. Therefore, we cannot ignore our own responsibilities and blame the consequences on the gods. Such arrogant blame is extremely unreasonable, but it is a common practice in our society. Many people do not understand the meaning of cause and effect, and habitually blame others for their difficulties and mistakes. This ignorant practice is one way in which maintaining a corrupt view leads to harm and prevents spiritual development.

Egotistical Views

When people cling to egotistical views, they become self-centered and judgmental. They believe their way of thinking is the ultimate truth, and everyone else is wrong. They are stubborn and cannot tolerate anyone who disagrees with them. Even when they know they are wrong, some people try to maintain their position by irrationally insisting that they are right. They defend and try to strengthen their weak argument by insulting and defaming others. This egotistical attitude disguises falsehood as truth, corruption as righteousness, and depravity as virtue; it is erroneous and extremely dangerous.

Views That Misuse the Precepts

When people possess erroneous views of the precepts, they cling to beliefs that are inconsistent with the Dharma and thereby misuse the teachings. This is usually in the hope of gaining worldly blessings and justifying improper actions. Typically, these people are arrogant and self-righteous. They see themselves as members of a superior breed and often attempt to elevate their status above others'. Unfortunately, their claims and deeds may be convincing, and many people fall victim to their acts and blindly follow and worship them.

Several years ago, a newspaper reported that a woman lived in seclusion for one hundred days without food and water. The news that she came out of seclusion looking strong and robust caught the attention of the media, and some people began to worship her as a living goddess. Upon further examination, the story was found to be full of holes. Can a person survive without food and water? Even plants need sun and water. Survival despite the absence of these essentials contradicts the laws of nature. Whether a person is cultivated or not does not depend on superficial and contrived actions, but rather on the purity of intentions within the heart and mind, and resulting practice. Misusing precepts in order to gain publicity and fame is an example of an erroneous, and therefore damaging, view of the precepts.

Not only do erroneous views cloud our wisdom, they can also cost us our lives and trap us in the cycle of suffering. We cannot underscore the importance of this enough. How can we avoid erroneous views and cultivate the right view and understanding? This is a very important first step in our Buddhist practice. However, in order to answer this question, we first need to discuss briefly what is meant by the term "worldly views." Like erroneous views, worldly views keep us distant from the truth and, sadly, keep the Dharma hidden and perplexing.

WORLDLY VIEWS

There are as many ways of looking at the world as there are creatures under the sun. Nevertheless, for the purpose of studying harmful perspectives rooted in worldly views, I present the following four major categories: pleasure in the five desires and six dusts, fulfillment in individual accomplishments and merits, limits of a one-hundred-year lifespan, and seeking truth in superstitious practices.

The Worldly Find Pleasure in the Five Desires and the Six Dusts

Most people find happiness in material pleasures of the senses and tirelessly chase after fulfillment through sensory experience. This type of external pleasure, however, is only illusory; the inner peace of the heart and mind is true joy. There are many millionaires who have beautiful spouses, enormous mansions, and fancy cars, but they do not know how to experience the real meaning of life and truth. The pursuit of external satisfaction leaves them out of touch with their true nature. They may possess the world, but they remain internally impoverished and shallow. In the world, there are many such poor, rich men and women.

According to the sutras, the pleasure found in the *five desires* (wealth, beauty, fame, food, and sleep) and the *six dusts* (sight, sound, smell, taste, touch, and ideas) is incomplete and impure. This form of pleasure is flawed, because by its transient nature it can never lead to ultimate truth and joy. It is impure because it is self-centered and can give rise to distress and pain. It is fleeting and impermanent, causing a perpetual cycle of scarcity and abundance; to have is bliss, to lose is agony.

Those who indulge in eating and sexual gratification without self-control are like moths that die upon flying into lamps. They trap themselves in the depths of pain and despair without realizing the causes of their destruction. Worldly pleasure is like a honey-dipped sword; it may taste sweet, but it can also cause considerable damage and pain. We should cultivate our wisdom to see through the illusive nature of material and worldly pleasures. Ultimately, true satisfaction can only come about through pursuing the limitless Dharma and delighting in its purity.

The Worldly Find Fulfillment in Individual Accomplishments and Merits

While some people may not be drawn to material pleasures, they are still attracted to fame and glory. Their goal in life is to leave their mark on history. Certainly, we should all strive for success and accomplishment; however, we should realize that worldly achievement exists merely on a superficial level. We should not lose sight of the fact that maintaining a healthy mind and body, achieving higher moral character, perceiving the universe with the right view, and understanding ultimate reality are much more worthwhile goals.

Many times I have heard people say, "Since the purpose of religion is to teach us to do good, I really have no need for religion as long as my values are sound." Actually, this is a very limited idea. The completeness of human life requires more conditions and elements than personal morality. The Dharma is not just about attaining individual liberation through doing good and abstaining from evil. The Dharma also tells us how to help others, as well as ourselves, embark on the path of happiness and freedom. Extending compassion and spiritual cultivation to others and ourselves is the meaning and value of religion. Once we have an ethical foundation, we should develop an altruistic spirit and dedicate ourselves to helping all sentient beings free themselves from suffering. Why should we limit ourselves to individual accomplishments and a system of isolated, personal morality? If our accomplishments are driven by a desire for individual satisfaction, then even though we make a name for ourselves in history, our accomplishments will not amount to anything great. Our fame will be self-serving and righteous. We should develop our *bodhicitta* and dedicate ourselves to the welfare of all beings. Only then will we be on the path to realizing life's full potential, manifested through the expansion of our individual potential and the potential of other people.

The Worldly Find Longevity in a One-Hundred-Year Lifespan

Most of us want to live a long life. We may even wish to live to be one hundred. Medical advances have made it possible to extend the average human lifespan. Additionally, we have offspring to carry on the family name, which represents another attempt to extend our lives. But how many years does longevity actually entail? When someone lives to be one hundred, we throw a big party and everyone celebrates. Is a lifespan of one hundred years really that long? For someone whose desire is insatiable, one hundred years may feel much too short.

Even a lifespan as long as that of the legendary Peng Zhu, who lived to be eight hundred years old, is very short when compared with that of the universe. In terms of worldly perceptions and existence, would life truly be wonderful if we were to live to be one hundred? We can imagine what it would be like. The children and grandchildren of a centenarian would probably be aged seniors in their eighties and sixties, respectively. A centenarian may even have to bear the sorrow of outliving his or her own children and grandchildren. What happiness can we speak of then? From a worldly perspective, longevity can be the cause of additional pain and sadness. With our vision failing and our health deteriorating in old age, days could drag out like years if we are not grounded mentally and dedicated to the correct understanding of the Dharma. With a correct understanding of the Dharma, one can have a correct view of longevity.

A devotee once asked a Chan master to pray for his longevity. The master asked, "How many more years do you wish to live?"

The devotee replied, "I am now sixty. I will have no regrets if I can live for another twenty years. It is such a blessing to live to eighty."

"You only want twenty more years! It will go by in no time. You can ask for more."

The bewildered devotee asked, "I can ask for more? In that case, make it forty more years. I will live to the incredible age of one hundred!"

"Forty, even one hundred years, will disappear like a flash of lightning. It will all be over in the blink of the eye. You should ask for much, much more."

The devotee was stupefied. Slowly, he asked, "In your opinion, should I ask for a few thousand, or maybe even ten thousand years?"

"No, you should ask for an immeasurable lifespan."

We should seek a boundless and immeasurable life—an eternally birthless and deathless true life—and not limit ourselves to a fleeting worldly lifespan of a few decades or a century. The value of life is not in how long we live, but in how we live our lives. Is our focus on worldly existence or spiritual nurturance? If we can live life to its fullest meaning, then even an instant of living is eternity.

The Worldly Find Truth in Superstitious Practices

Some people believe that the Dharma is based on superstition; what they do not realize is that it is actually our daily living that is full of superstitious practices. We often celebrate weddings or birthdays with a feast, slaughtering many animals just to satisfy our appetite. In the course of celebrating life, we take the lives of many animals for selfish and ritualistic purposes. Similarly, in the course of marking the union of two people, we tear apart the families of many animals. Such acts are totally inconsistent with the idea of celebration and run contrary to the spirit of compassion.

According to Chinese custom, some people settle their arguments by going to the temple and making an oath with the decapitation of a chicken. The commitment of an oath should come from within and thus be reflected in our actions. How can the decapitation of a chicken bind us to our promises? Moreover, all life is precious. What right do we have to take the life of another being just for our own convenience and advancement? If a person thinks he or she can show conviction with a chicken head, I truly wonder about his or her integrity and correct view of the Dharma.

Some people depend on their gods for too much. For example, when they face a difficult decision, they ask their gods for guidance. When they become sick, they try to heal themselves by smearing their bodies with the ashes of incense. When they confront hard times, they burn paper money in the hope that their troubles will vanish. Their fervency in religious practice is to be applauded, but their method of going about it blindly, indiscriminately, and with reliance on external deeds is questionable. We should know that our faith in the Dharma should start from reverence, the willingness to cultivate a deeper understanding, and the spirit of giving selflessly to others. Giving is not just limited to material giving. If our circumstances enable us to give, we should devote our energy and resources toward furthering our religious cultivation and benefiting the community. It is only by pursuing truth, acting compassionately, and offering blessings and merits for the benefit of others that we can ensure bountiful results in our spiritual development.

While worldly views and perceptions may look appealing, they do not hold up to closer examination. People often embrace views not because they are credible or sound, but merely because they are held by the majority. Actually, the reason we all accept and adhere to these worldly views is the persistence of our unclear minds—a direct result of ignorance clouding our pure nature. But, if we diligently polish and clean our minds, one day they will shine, and we will become enlightened. The truth of the Dharma will become perfectly clear. In this state, we will walk in the company of Buddhas and bodhisattvas and live in the total delight of true freedom.

LEVELS OF PERCEPTION AND UNDERSTANDING

Serving as a Friend to the Buddha, the Dharma, and the Sangha

In striving to understand Buddhist perception and understanding on a more profound level, one should know how to support and protect the Dharma. This serves as a foundation for practice that offers compassion and ultimately succeeds in the eradication of suffering for all beings. Let us examine the meaning of the term "Dharma Friend" and the levels on which Buddhist practitioners can protect the Dharma through expanding their perception of Buddhist teachers, temples, and salvation. As our levels of spiritual practice develop, so do our levels of perception and understanding.

I begin every speech addressing all the Buddhists in the audience as "Dharma Friends." What does the term "Dharma Friends" really mean? Do we Buddhists really understand the depth and meet the criteria of this term? The term "Dharma Friends" means that we are friends and guardians of the Dharma and the Buddhist religion. When we do not have a correct understanding of the term "Dharma Friends," we will inevitably make many mistakes in the way we try to embody its meaning.

What does the term "Dharma Friends" encompass? Let me illustrate the meaning by showing how spiritual practice develops through stages of understanding. On the most primary level are people who, while they are faithful, fail to discern the Dharma from a cultist practice. They idolize and blindly worship strange and supernatural phenomena just because these phenomena are unusual and supposedly beyond the worldly realm. Then there are people who, while claiming to follow the Dharma, actually practice their faith only for worldly gain and blessings. They pray to their god or gods for wealth and longevity. They do not realize that the true meaning of practice lies in compassionate giving and helping. There are also some people who, while they are able to take the first steps towards practicing the Dharma, become attached to one particular teacher just because the teacher was kind to them. But the sutras say, "Follow the Dharma, not the [Dharma] teacher." It is easy to get caught up with a person who has a charismatic personality, but only the Dharma will not lead us astray.

To follow the Dharma is to practice the Dharma as realized by the Buddha and upheld by the sangha. The Dharma encompasses the unchanging truth of the universe. These teachings are timeless and are as relevant today as when they were first taught by the Buddha. Only when we allow the Dharma to be our guide can our minds become pure and our lives become sublime. An individual teacher is subject to the insecurities and impermanence of the world; people come and go, and are limited by the nature of the human body. Resting our faith on one person is like relying on the morning dew, which disappears under the sun; it is unreliable and changes under altered conditions. Thus, it is not enough for Buddhists to support Dharma teachers alone; we must also support, protect and share the

Dharma. This is the fundamental duty and joy of being a Dharma Friend.

Even though we may have admiration and respect for a certain Dharma teacher, we should also extend support to all the men, women, and children who study, follow, and spread the Buddha's teachings. We should generously give our love to all beings, because the sutras say that Buddhism is found within the community. The Buddha also told his disciples, "I, too, am a member of the community." A person who serves the sangha has Buddha in his heart and extends the wisdom of Buddha's teachings. The one who supports others in their practice of the Dharma and who earnestly strives to deliver all beings from suffering is indeed a true Dharma Friend; he or she is a true guardian of Buddhism.

Some Buddhists have special admiration for a particular teacher; others give their full support to particular temples. While we remain committed to a certain teacher or temple, we should also support and honor all other accomplished teachers and lend our support to all temples that uphold the Dharma and serve the public. With compassion, we should help every monastery practicing the altruistic Mahayana spirit of universal salvation, embracing all practitioners striving to know the Dharma. We Buddhists should expand our support for an individual teacher to the larger community of practitioners, for a single temple to support for all places of practice, and from the path of individual salvation to the salvation of all beings. All Dharma Friends should aspire to support, practice, and spread Buddhism in this manner.

Stages of Practice

Just as there are many levels at which one can be a guardian or friend of the Dharma, there are also many reasons why a person may want to learn about Buddhism, resulting in corresponding levels of Buddhist practice. Some beginners only wish to amass a fortune or to have a bountiful and harmonious family, so they work diligently and are generous and charitable. Their rewards, however, are limited to worldly blessings in the human realm, for this is where their thoughts and actions are focused. In such cases, the foundation of practice is unstable, for these people are still under the control of worldly habits and views. Their progress is slow and does not come easily. This is the first level of Buddhist practice.

Some people realize the superficial and illusive nature of worldly pleasures. They choose to renounce the traditional household life and seek the joy of ultimate truth. This is the second level of Buddhist practice. There is no question that renunciation is uplifting for one's life and character, but beyond self-liberation, one should also be concerned with the happiness and relief from suffering of *all* beings. Thus, in addition to renouncing household life, one may also take the bodhisattva vow to propagate Buddhist teachings and deliver all sentient beings. This is a higher form of Buddhist practice.

In Buddhism, there are five stages of cultivation, which are commonly referred to as "The Ways of the Five Vehicles." According to the order described in The Ways of the Five Vehicles, we should first learn to uphold the Five Precepts of the "human vehicle," from which we move on to the Ten Virtuous Practices of the "celestial vehicle." When we have internalized these practices, we then learn and practice the Four Noble Truths of the "sravaka vehicle" and the Twelve Links of Conditioned Genesis of the "pratyeka-buddha vehicle." Finally, we should cultivate the Six Paramitas of the "Bodhisattva vehicle," benefiting and fulfilling ourselves while doing the same for others. Although sravakas and pratyeka-buddhas are enlightened beings and their cultivation transcends the ordinary, they are focused upon individual, rather than universal salvation. It is only when we have the compassion described in the saying, "We wish for the liberation of all beings from pain and will not seek comfort just for ourselves," that we can work for the benefit of all beings in the bodhisattva spirit. With this compassion we can help others in a transcendental yet worldly way, and reach the highest form of Buddhist realization.

As described above, the five stages of cultivation are the human, celestial, sravaka, pratyeka-buddha, and bodhisattva vehicles. The bodhisattva vehicle can be further subdivided into forty-one stages, or fifty-two according to another classification. Just as there are stages of cultivation, the perception and understanding of the ultimate reality of each of these five vehicles is also different. The *Diamond Sutra*, the *Heart Sutra*, and the *Mahaprajnaparamita Sastra* also tell us that in accordance with our spiritual maturation and the merit of our pure intentions, our realization of *prajna* (wisdom) and *sunyata* (emptiness) is different at each of these stages.

In the case of humans and celestial beings, prajna is the cultivation of correct perception and understanding. From the stages of human and celestial being to the stages of sravaka and pratyeka-buddha, prajna is the understanding of the truth of conditioned genesis. When one's horizon is expanded to where one has the welfare of all sentient beings in one's heart, one ventures into the realm of the Mahayana bodhisattva. One will then see the fundamental law of the universe—the truth of emptiness. This is prajna for the stage of bodhisattva, and bodhisattvas apply this prajna in limitless ways to help others. The stage of Buddha is reached when we can see the reality of our pure original nature, the Buddha Nature. This is the highest and most wondrous form of prajna.

The many stages of realization include the right view, the law of conditioned genesis, the truth of sunyata, and the ultimate realization of prajna. These stages are sometimes classified as the wisdom of action, the wisdom of insight, the wisdom of equality, and the wisdom of the wondrous mirror. Regardless of which classification we use, the most important aspect to remember is that the distinction between these stages is based on our intentions and the way we practice in our hearts and minds. We should not dwell upon the artificial classification we impose on them.

How can we heighten the value of existence? How do we reach the highest and most wondrous realm of practice? How can we be in the Buddha's world of great kindness and compassion? How can we venture into the bodhisattva's sea of prajna? These are urgent and pressing questions that we cannot afford to ignore. In the next section, we further examine specific practices that help us take footsteps on the path of ultimate compassion, ultimate freedom, and ultimate truth.

PERCEPTION AND UNDERSTANDING IN BUDDHISM

What constitutes right perception and understanding? We must understand Buddha's teachings on the "right view," for these are the keys in our search for the ultimate truth. Some Buddhists, when faced with problems, obstacles, or misfortune, give up their practice and lose their faith in Buddhism. As mentioned earlier, sometimes they even criticize the religion and complain that the Buddhas and bodhisattvas fail to bless them. Such an attitude stems from the lack of the right perception and understanding. To have the right view is to have faith in our beliefs and not suffer a severe spiritual upheaval during difficult times. When tested, the right view will help us to remain strong, maintain our beliefs, stand up for the benefit of the community, and fearlessly spread the words of truth without reservation. The right view is to understand that there is goodness and evil in the world, that there are causes and effects, past lives and future lives, and worldly and transcendental beings. When we understand these truths, we will then know the importance of being mindful of our deeds, words, and thoughts. We know that if we are to avoid falling into the three suffering realms, we have to do good and refrain from evil.

The Buddha also teaches us the Fourfold Mindfulness, the Four Rules to Observe, the Three Dharma Seals, and the Noble Eightfold Path. These practices all constitute the right view and are well presented in Buddhist sutras. A brief summary of each of these teachings follows.

The Fourfold Mindfulness

The Fourfold Mindfulness is also called The Four Areas of Mindfulness. This doctrine describes areas where we should always anchor our mind. We should be mindful that "the body is impure," "sensations will always result in suffering," "the mind is impermanent," and "all phenomena are without a nature of their own." From suffering, sunyata, and selflessness, the Fourfold Mindfulness helps us see the truth of life and the universe.

As discussed earlier, because many of us perceive the body to be real and permanent, we spend much time and energy nurturing and adorning it. Being mindful that the body is impure because of its impermanence helps us to break our attachment to the body, the source of our many desires. If we can see through the illusiveness of our physical bodies, we will free ourselves to pursue the true and unchanging Dharma body (i.e., the body of teachings) and prajna-wisdom. Though suffering is more predominant in life than happiness, we still act out of ignorance by pursuing sensory pleasure, and in so doing we create more negative karma. We fail to realize that our focus must be finding happiness in spiritual cultivation and helping others, instead of insisting on heightening sensations and, consequently, heightening suffering.

Our mind is like a waterfall; it never stops running. Mental constructs and ideas surface and disappear as fast as they appear in a rapid and eternal cycle. When we are not mindful that "the mind is impermanent," we let our minds become dangerously attached to what we perceive as an unchanging idea.

All phenomena of the world are impermanent and without an independent nature of their own; nothing is ever static and unchanging, or immune to causes and conditions. If we do not know how to let go and if we remain attached to the self or to other phenomena, suffering will invariably follow. However, if we can perceive and understand the world through the practice of the Fourfold Mindfulness, our minds and bodies will be forever pure and free.

The Four Rules to Observe

The four rules that we should observe are: "Follow the Dharma, not the teacher," "Follow the meaning, not the words," "Follow wisdom, not knowledge," and "Follow the ultimate truth, not apparent truths." Earlier, we discussed the meaning of "Follow the Dharma, not the teacher." What it essentially tells us is to follow the truth of the Buddha's teachings, which is eternal and unchanging, rather than the teacher, who is impermanent and changing.

"Follow the meaning, not the words" means that we should understand the true purpose of the teachings rather than interpret them improperly, engage in frivolous arguments, or play word games manipulating meaning to suit ulterior purposes. "Follow wisdom, not knowledge" reminds us that we should live under the guidance of prajna wisdom rather than worldly perception and knowledge. "Follow the ultimate truth, not apparent truths" means that we should follow the ultimate truth of the universe and not blindly follow heresies or superstitions just for the sake of convenience. These Four Rules to Observe are our compass in discovering the truth of life and the universe. They are the gateway to the treasure of freedom.

The Three Dharma Seals

The "Three Dharma Seals" is an important doctrine of Buddhism; it embodies the truth of life and the universe. The

Three Dharma Seals are as follows: "All *samskaras* (composite things) are impermanent," "All dharmas do not have an independent self," and "Nirvana is perfect peace."

All samskaras are impermanent: All phenomena, words, and deeds in this world are impermanent and forever changing. Life is impermanent; even the world is impermanent. All worldly phenomena and dharmas are impermanent. Clinging to the idea or hope that something will remain permanent and unchanged results in a fruitless quest for peace, happiness and understanding. Only when we rid ourselves of worldly assumptions can we attain the transcendental world of true permanence.

All dharmas do not have an independent self: There is nothing in this world that is unchanging and immune to decay. Like our bodies, wealth, fame, relationships, and everything else will not last forever; sooner or later, these things will all leave us. Thus, if we understand that all things arise within a certain field of conditions and that all things cease when these conditions no longer exist, we will not be attached to worldly phenomena—for they are impermanent and cannot arise or exist independently. Nothing comes into being on its own, but only as a result of its relationship to other beings or phenomena. Understanding this, we will rest our bodies and minds in the realm of non-arising and non-ceasing. In this way, we will savor the ultimate joy of living, and not fear change or even death.

Nirvana is perfect peace: The world of nirvana is a pure and ultimately blissful world. Within nirvana, there is only peace; there is no pain or distress. Although the Buddha considered entering the non-arising and non-ceasing realm of nirvana after enlightenment, for the sake of all beings he compassionately decided to stay in this world and give us his teachings. Those who consider liberation from rebirth as the sole purpose of Buddhism have a passive and detached perspective. They do not fully understand the Buddha's teachings, for nirvana does not mean for us to distance ourselves from all beings and to live in isolation from others. The Buddha rebuked such people as "rotten seeds." The ultimate realm of nirvana is not total extinction or annihilation. It is the peace of non-attachment and can be described with these words: "With great wisdom, one does not cling to birth and death. With great compassion, one does not cling to nirvana." Because nirvana is the perfect and transcendent balance between wisdom and compassion, those who attain nirvana are able to continually deliver sentient beings and never need a moment of rest.

The Noble Eightfold Path

The Noble Eightfold Path gives us understanding of the Four Noble Truths—the truth of suffering, the truth of the arising of suffering, the truth of cessation of suffering, and the truth of the path leading to the cessation of suffering. This understanding comes through right view, right thought, right speech, right action, right livelihood, right effort, right mindfulness, and right concentration.

From right view, which is the basis of the Noble Eightfold Path, we proceed to right thought, in which our thoughts are only loving, selfless, and nonviolent. Right thought nurtures our wisdom, or prajna, and influences our actions. Right speech teaches us to be mindful of the karmic consequences of speech and to abstain from lying, abusive language, and idle chatter. Right action is to refrain from all unethical and unwholesome acts, and to actively perform good deeds that honor the precepts and benefit others. Right livelihood means that we should live our lives in accordance with the Buddha's teaching. Right effort is to have the commitment and dedication to practice the path of nirvana. Right mindfulness is to use wisdom to be mindful of this Noble Path. Finally, right concentration is to focus our thoughts and nurture wholesome mental states through meditative concentration.

In summary, this Noble Eightfold Path is a tool that can help us to refrain from what is evil and wrong; thus it is described as "noble." This practice can help us to reach the realm of nirvana; thus it is called a "path." If we can be steadfast in our practice of the Noble Eightfold Path, we have, indeed, the right perception and understanding in its truest form.

In addition to the above, I would like to touch on another correct perception and understanding of Buddhist practices: the Pure Land practice of being continually mindful of Amitabha Buddha. Some people may remain skeptical and ask, "Chanting the name of Amitabha Buddha is for old ladies. What can it really do?" Some people even ask incredulously, "How can one be liberated from rebirth simply by being mindful of Amitabha Buddha and chanting his name?" Others may wonder, "How can the words 'Amitabha Buddha' help us to reach the Pure Land of Ultimate Bliss and attain a boundless life?" Actually, the purpose of this Pure Land practice is more than simply liberation from rebirth. It takes us deeper into our practice and teaches us to see the reality of existence.

Once, someone asked a master, "Can chanting the name 'Amitabha Buddha' truly yield amazing results?"

This was a difficult question to answer, but the master had a skillful reply. He looked at the person and reprimanded him, "What an idiot!"

The man's shock at the master's reply quickly turned into anger. Rolling up his sleeves and clenching his fists, the man yelled at the master, "How dare you call me names?"

With a knowing smile, the master replied, "See, just the word 'idiot' has the impact of changing your state of mind. Why can't the words 'Amitabha Buddha' be just as powerful?"

Therefore, even though our lives may be hectic, Buddhists should practice chanting the name of Amitabha Buddha. The Pure Land practice was espoused by Chan Master Yongming Yenshou, who said, "The myriad who cultivate [this practice] is the same myriad who will reach [the Pure Land]." Let us pray that Amitabha Buddha will help us attain the correct perception and understanding regarding this practice and, in doing so, help us find the strength to reach the Pure Land.

Chapter Two

TIME AND SPACE

One of the fundamental perceptions in Buddhism concerns the understanding of time and space. Time traverses the past, present and future. Space spans hundreds and thousands of realms, spreading across all ten directions. For most living beings, time and space are like the act of breathing: we breathe every moment, yet we are not conscious of this action. Depending on our individual histories and experiences, we all have different perceptions, expectations, and attitudes regarding time and space. For example, certain insects live for a day and are content; humans live to eighty and are still not satisfied. They hunger for more time on this earth. We all confine ourselves to our own limited slice of time and space, encasing ourselves in illusive boundaries. From the Buddhist perspective of samsara (the cycle of rebirth), the lifespan of all sentient beings is limitless. Time as well as space is endless and thus cannot be measured. If we penetrate the ultimate truth of time and space, we can be liberated from the space defined by the four directions of north, east, south, and west and emerge from the time constraints of seconds, minutes, days, and months. We will then be in the dimension of total freedom, and we will be able to experience what is described in the saying, "Clear, cool water everywhere; prajna flowers every moment." I turn now to a more in-depth discussion of four key aspects of the Buddhist perspective on time and space.

TIME AND SPACE FOR ALL LIVING BEINGS

The term "all living beings" includes not only human beings but also beings in the other five realms of existence: celestial beings, asuras, animals, hungry ghosts,[1] and beings in the hell realms. What is time and space for all living beings within these six realms of existence? We will first examine time.

Ksana

In Buddhism, a "ksana" is the smallest unit of time. Within the context of how we measure time today, it is approximately one seventy-fifth of a second. A ksana is extremely brief. In Buddhism, how do we gauge such a short duration of time? A reflection is a moment of thought; 90 ksanas pass in one human reflection. Within one ksana, there are 900 instances of arising and ceasing. There are 32,820,000 ksanas in one day.

These descriptions demonstrate that the arising and ceasing within a ksana occurs very rapidly. At any particular moment, we see flowers as red and leaves as green. In reality, they change dramatically in every ksana, and after a while, they will wilt. Within each ksana, they are perpetually growing and wilting in a kaleidoscope of color and texture. Take the example of a table: we observe it standing firmly. However, if we were to examine it under an electron microscope, we would see that the internal fiber structure of the wood is changing, expanding and contracting as it decays from ksana to ksana. In a few years, this table will no longer function with its original integrity. In

---

1. A "hungry ghost" is a denizen of one of the miserable planes of existence. Hungry ghosts are unable to find rebirth in an embodied form.

this world, how can there be any flowers or leaves or grass that will never wilt? How can there be any tables, chairs, or beds that will not be subject to destruction? All phenomena and all existence arise from ksana to ksana; therefore, all phenomena and existence cease from ksana to ksana. There is a saying, "When a young man snaps his fingers, sixty-three ksanas have gone by." From this perspective, time passes very quickly. Youth can disappear in an instant.

Asamkhya Kalpa

In Buddhism, a very long period of time is called an "asamkhya kalpa." It is an inconceivably vast length of time. The duration of an asamkhya kalpa is so long that any attempts to describe it in words would be difficult and inadequate. A discussion about two lesser units of time within an asamkhya kalpa may provide a more reasonable reference point for understanding the magnitude of this concept of limitlessness.

Mustard seed kalpa: Imagine if we were to take a huge container measuring ten kilometers on each side and fill it with mustard seeds. Then, every one hundred years, we would remove one seed. The time it would take to empty the container of all the mustard seeds is one "mustard seed kalpa." Exactly how long a mustard seed kalpa is would probably have to be determined with the help of several computers.

Boulder kalpa: Imagine if we were to take a huge boulder measuring ten kilometers on each side, and sand the boulder with a piece of sandpaper once every hundred years. The time it would take to reduce the boulder to dust is one "boulder kalpa." This period of time is much longer than that of a mustard seed kalpa.

Within the Buddhist time scale, both the mustard seed kalpa and the boulder kalpa are only considered minor kalpas. In contrast, the duration of a major kalpa, such as the asamkhya kalpa, is so immeasurable and infinite that it is beyond words.

The Lifespan of Living Beings

Never in the course of our lives, or the lives of any beings, is there a still moment. Like bubbles on the surface of water, lives arise as suddenly as they disappear, each spanning a different length of time. Human beings typically can live to approximately a hundred; some insects are born at dawn and are dead by dusk. To such an insect, one day is the equivalent of one hundred years in human terms. Tortoises, the longest-living creatures on earth, can live up to two hundred and fifty years. Elephants and dolphins can live to be ninety. Cows, horses, monkeys, and dogs generally live fifteen to twenty years. Rats may live for three to four years, and flies and mosquitoes can only live for a period of about seven days. Viruses usually perish in less than three hours. Although there is an enormous difference between three hours and two hundred fifty years, nevertheless, each existence spans a lifetime.

The lifespan of a living being—whether it is a day, a few hours, a century, or two hundred and fifty years—may seem lengthy to some, by worldly standards. However, in the unlimited extent of time and space, these lengths of time are quite brief. Why? According to Buddhist scriptures, there are beings with much longer lifespans than human beings and that even far surpass the impressive lifespans of tortoises. The realm above humans is the celestial realm consisting of many heavens. The heaven closest to us is called the "Caturmaharaja Heaven." Beings in Caturmaharaja Heaven can live up to five hundred celestial years, or 25,000 human years. Above that is the "Trayastrimsat Heaven." Beings in Trayastrimsat Heaven can live to 50,000 human years. Beings in "Yama Heaven" have lifespans of around 400,000 human years. Beings in "Tusita Heaven" live for about 1,600,000 human years. Beings in the yet higher "Nirmanarati Heaven" can live for as long as 6,400,000 human years. Beyond the heavens, in the realm of desire, are the heavens within the realm of forms. The length of the lifespan there is beyond our comprehension. Within the heaven of forms is the "Paranirmita-vasavartin Heaven." Beings there can live to the equivalent of 25,600,000 human years. Such long lifespans challenge our imagination. Beyond the heavens in the realm of forms are the heavens in the realm of formlessness. Beings in this realm can live to 80,000 major kalpas. The duration of such a lifespan is incomprehensible. Regardless of how long these beings live, they are nonetheless still trapped in the cycle of rebirth. They still cannot transcend the boundary of time and space.

Conversely, there are equally as expansive durations of time below the human existence. For example, time in the "Avici Hell" stretches out endlessly. The inhabitants of Avici Hell, the hungry ghosts, suffer tremendously. Their ever-expanding bodies and their ever-conscious minds experience relentless torments. The suffering from incessant punishment and unfulfilled greed are beyond imagination. The sutras give the following example of "a hungry ghost waiting for spittle." There was a hungry ghost in hell who had been starving for years and years. As he had not eaten anything for a long time, his hunger was unbearable. Consumed by his greed, he painfully yearned for anything to eat. Eventually, he spotted a person who was about to spit. He eagerly waited for this person to spit so that he could consume the spittle and relieve his desperation. He waited and waited. During the time he was waiting, he saw a city crumble and then be rebuilt seven times. Immeasurable time passed before he finally got the spittle. In hell, where there is no day or night, time inches forward at an agonizing pace.

Society's common definition of time is merely a fraction of the truth of boundless and endless time. It is not easy to comprehend the vast and immeasurable proportions of time, but it is essential in our quest for ultimate liberation.

Let us now examine space. In Buddhism, the largest unit of

space is called a "Buddhaksetra" or Buddha Land, and the smallest unit of space is called a "suksma" or dust grain. Despite their different names, both terms ultimately describe the three thousand chiliocosms, which is endless, immeasurable, unlimited, and unbounded.

How big is the universe? Modern astronomy research indicates that the planet Earth is only 1/1,300,000th the size of the sun. The sun, in turn, is only one among millions of stars in the Milky Way galaxy. The universe itself probably has hundreds of millions of galaxies like the Milky Way. How can we possibly imagine the immense proportions of the universe?

On the other end of the scale, modern physics analyzes matter in smaller and smaller particles called atoms, protons, electrons, and neutrons. A suksma is even smaller than a neutron. This tiny unit of space is tens of thousands times smaller than anything we commonly know. Our little finger may look clean and spotless, yet it actually harbors millions of dust particles and microorganisms. Each eye of a housefly consists of four thousand lenses. Such spatial dimension is so minute that it is undetectable by the naked human eye, and a suksma is even beyond the reach of a microscope.

With the help of modern laboratory equipment, technology has provided us with a broad and detailed understanding of the time and space in which we live. When we study these modern findings based on scientific research, we realize that the universe is indeed extremely vast and deep. However, the dimensions offered by these discoveries are small and shallow when we consider time and space from the Buddhist perspective. Why? In Buddhism, time and space are immense, without an outer limit, and yet minuscule, without an inner limit. Time and space are immeasurable and boundless, for the Dharma is forever beyond the limits of time and space. This is more evident today than ever before, since I may give a speech that can instantly be televised to all of Taiwan. The following day, it can be translated and distributed to the world in printed form. In an instant, it can be transmitted around the globe by computer technology. In the future, it can be published as a book to build Dharma connections with tens of millions of people everywhere in the world. Considering the limitlessness of time and space, how quickly and how far might the Dharma be spread in the future?

THE PRACTICAL REALITY OF TIME AND SPACE

In the vast universe, our daily lives are intimately connected with time and space; they can never be separated. The level of success people achieve and the effectiveness with which people handle their affairs depend on their utilization of time and their allocation of space. Our awareness of time and space and the choices we make based on this awareness directly influence the harmony or discord of our interpersonal relationships. Without effective timing, we either move too quickly or too slowly, and can bring about the resentment or impatience of others. Without proper spatial awareness and sensitivity, we often invade others' space or rob them of their advantageous locations. Such ignorance of temporal and spatial dimensions can annoy and burden others. Thus, time and space have significant impact on our daily existence.

In today's society, some people never seem to have enough time; to them, every second passes with frustrating swiftness, and they are always greedy for more. There are others whose time passes painfully slowly; to them, days feel like years that drag on without mercy. Some people are impoverished and homeless, claiming one small square of a sidewalk as their domain. Others possess so much land and so many buildings that it seems they even want to own a piece of the moon. There are many different types of people and circumstances. The famous poet Tang Bohu once wrote about how fleeting and illusive time is:

Life rarely reaches seventy;
That I am seventy is a surprise.
I was too young the first ten years
And too old the last ten.
There are only fifty years in between;
Half of that time is spent at night.
By calculation I have only lived twenty-five years,
During which I have endured much toil and trouble.

Time is inherently impartial. The poor do not receive a minute less; the rich are not granted a second more. Time cannot be hoarded through even the strongest power or the most intense effort.

Time is a keen judge, as described in the saying, "A long journey can truly test a horse; the passage of time can reveal one's true character." Right or wrong, love or hatred, success or failure—all of these will be revealed in time. Time is also the arbiter of character, since a person's character, whether noble or base, will become evident over time.

Time exists in a threefold dimension in our everyday lives regardless of whether we believe that life rarely reaches seventy or that life begins at seventy. The lifespans of living beings gradually flow by in the threefold dimension of time: the past, present, and future. The past is quietly gone; it will never return. The present flies like an arrow and disappears in an instant. The future, amidst our lack of awareness and reverence for each moment, slowly draws closer and closer, until it suddenly slips by. Poets have often tried to describe the ephemeral and illusive nature of time in their poems.

The only thing truly equal in this world is gray hair;
It does not overlook the heads of the rich.
—Du Mu of the Tang Dynasty

Do not complain that we age too easily.
Even mountains turn white sometimes.
—LUO QILAN OF THE QING DYNASTY

These simple verses suggest that time is always fair. Time ages everyone, regardless of whether you are rich or poor, strong or weak. Just as there are times when green mountains are blanketed with snow and frost, there will also be a day when we are crowned with gray:

We all gain a year on our birthdays;
The world does not single me out to make me old.
—LU YOU OF THE SONG DYNASTY

This verse gently presents the truth that we all will get old. Every second, every year, we age. The fleeting years of human life disappear amidst the sound of New Year cheers and fire-crackers. Buddhism talks of the cycle of rebirth and the impermanence of all things, which is eloquently captured in this poem by the poet Bai Juyi:

Regrettably my hair is like snow.
You are young and strong with the vitality of clouds.
To whichever youngster who looks down on me,
White hair will also come to you someday.

As students of the Buddhist teachings, we strive to cultivate ourselves diligently in order to realize bodhi (enlightenment) in infinite time and space. We need to embrace eternity within every instant and see the wondrous reality in each flower, each tree, each body of water, and each rock. We can then venture into the supreme and timeless realm of the Dharma.

Not only must we learn to break through the confines of time, we need to do likewise regarding space. Some people climb a mountain to claim ownership of its precious land. Others sail the ocean to claim rights to its deep waters. In countless disputes and lawsuits over property, people fight for space with selfish and abrasive attitudes. Sometimes living beings even fight with the dead for space, insisting that graveyards be renovated for the purpose of constructing houses. Not only do people engage in disputes over land, nations also battle over boundary lines to seize more space for their people. Almost all the wars in the world are fought over the amount of available living space. "Ten thousand acres of fertile farm land, but how much can one eat in a day? One thousand mansions, but one can only sleep in an eight-foot space." This saying illustrates that all space, both tangible and intangible, is ultimately illusive and fleeting. The rapidly existing and disintegrating space of the three realms (of desire, form, and formlessness) ultimately arises from the mind. Poet Bai Juyi expressed this concept well in the following poem:

Why fight over the space on the tip of a snail's antenna?
Our existence is only as fleeting as a flint spark.

Similarly, I often share the following saying with people: "Trees may live for a thousand years; glory and sorrow cannot last for more than a hundred." These lines advise us to let go of attachment, to let go of illusive forms. We should cultivate ourselves beyond the suffering of rebirth and impermanence, and in doing so, we will eventually abandon pain and attain happiness. Only then will we be liberated from our confining definitions of time and space.

In our daily lives, there are many examples when time and space are simply unbearable. We are often rendered desperate, pained and hopeless. Some of the worst moments are described in the following traditional folk song:

Rendered destitute and the bank is closed;
Sad and sick in bed;
Wronged with no outlet for grievance;
Disappointed and lovesick;
On the day of a fatal diagnosis;
Escaped convicts with nowhere to hide;
Impoverished with nowhere to turn;
One's spouse and children crying in sorrow.

Another popular song poignantly describes more of these moments:

One waits for one's date at sunset, yet the lovely one fails to
   show;
One takes an entrance exam, but one's name does not make
   the list;
One faces farewells and death, and one cries from heartbreak;
One is about to become a new mother, yet the pains of labor
   are unrelenting;
One tosses and turns in bed, yet one cannot fall asleep;
One has teenagers who love to fight, so one is worried sick;
One has terrible stomach cramps and needs fast relief, yet a
   bathroom is not to be found;
One tries one's best in a campaign, yet loses the election when
   the votes are counted;
One sees a motorcycle heading straight for one's car, so one
   tries to brake urgently;
One has been caught for violating the law, and this is the
   moment for announcing one's sentence;
One is a hundred meters into the battlefield, and one can nei-
   ther advance nor retreat;
One's family cannot get along, and one is in the midst of
   fighting and splitting up.

There are far too many dreadful examples of intolerable time and space. The situations mentioned above—being stood up, failing an examination, giving birth, being sick, being in a car accident, awaiting sentencing, couples fighting, facing farewells and deaths—can happen to any one of us. These situations can lead to monstrous arguments and endless disputes. This seat is mine; this item is mine; this parcel of land is mine, and you may not use any of it. You did not have time to talk to me because you were in a hurry; you still missed your flight by two minutes. You were upset about not getting on a ship in time until you found out that you escaped drowning in a shipwreck. Although our existence seems real, the time and space we live in are actually illusive like the reflection of the moon in the water.

Life Is Illusive like a Flower

During the time it takes for flowers to bloom and wilt, all of us are gradually growing old. Just as this year's blossoms are different from those of the previous year, I too am different from last year. All forms are equally illusive because they are constantly changing. The following three popular verses aptly describe this change:

The flowers of this year are as pretty as those of last year;
The person of this year is older than last year.
—GEN SHEN OF THE TANG DYNASTY

Fortune does not last for a thousand days;
Flowers cannot blossom for a hundred days;
If one does not treasure opportunities now,
One is left with nothing when they are gone.
—YUAN DYNASTY VERSE

On this day last year, at this threshold,
Your face and peach blossoms glowed together.
Now your lovely face is gone,
The peach blossoms still smile at the spring breeze.
—WANG MUQI OF THE SONG DYNASTY

Life Is Illusive like Flowing Water

In this world, only the ephemeral light born from the continuous ebb and flow of waves perseveres through time. A person's physical body cannot survive forever. Let me illustrate this point with the following two verses:

On the Yangzi River the waves from behind push the waves
    in front; a new generation replaces an older generation.
—TRADITIONAL FOLK SAYING

Water from the rear flows to the fore;
It has flowed like this from ancient time to the present.
The new persons are not the old ones,
They all walk across the bridge year after year.
—BAI JUYI OF THE TANG DYNASTY

Life Is Illusive like the Moon

From antiquity to the present, the same moon still shines. Our ancestors, having departed this world long ago, gazed at this very same celestial beauty. In the reality of human existence, who can be as everlasting as the moon? In fact, even the face of the moon changes between the new moon and full moon with the passage of time. Its constancy actually lies in its ever-changing appearance. With graceful thoughts and skillful pens, poets from the past to the present have written verses reflecting on the impermanence of human existence:

Modern people see not the ancient moon,
But the modern moon once shone upon ancient people.
—LI BAI OF THE TANG DYNASTY

By the riverbanks, who first sees the moon?
When does the moon above the river first shine upon a person?
Generation after generation, people's lives continue endlessly;
Year after year, the moon appears the same.
Not knowing for whom the moon is shining,
I only see the river flowing downstream.
—ZHANG RUOXU OF THE TANG DYNASTY

The time and space of human existence is like a flower, blossoming and wilting within a short time, and as illusive as the reflection of the moon in the water. I give many Dharma talks in lecture halls occupying space around the world. When the proper time comes, all of the guests leave. The lights are switched off and the sounds are silenced. When the doors are closed, the space that was once occupied by the hundreds or thousands of people sitting in the lecture halls will be vacated and returned to a state of quietude. Yet the Dharma relationships that were formed there remain at all times, accompanying each person on unique, but still entwined, journeys. All phenomena in this world may disappear like the faded flowers of yesterday. Only Dharma relationships are eternal, prevailing with the brilliance of an authentic gem beyond any conception of space or time. The Dharma lives forever.

THE LIBERATION OF BUDDHIST PRACTITIONERS FROM TIME AND SPACE

Countless masters in Buddhism have achieved the rewards of

spiritual cultivation. They are not hindered by hatred nor bound by attachment. They are relieved of suffering and ignorance. Liberated from the realm of time and space, they exist in total freedom. For these highly developed beings, time and space are vastly different from what they are to ordinary people who do not yet exist on an elevated spiritual plane.

These sages of Buddhism, being well cultivated in meditation, can stop the mind and calm the heart. They can venture into the profound, subtle, and wondrous realm of Dharmadhatu (the realm of the Dharma). They are able to penetrate the boundary of form and liberate themselves from the constraints of time and space. To them, according to a sutra, "A shortened ksana is not brief, and a lengthened asamkhya kalpa is not long." For example, Master Xu Yun, a Chan master in recent history, once retreated to Mt. Cuei Wei in Shanxi province. While waiting for the rice to cook, he decided to briefly meditate in a cave and quickly achieved samadhi, an advanced state of meditative concentration. When he emerged from his meditation, the rice was completely rotten. Eventually he realized that he had actually meditated for half a year, suspended in the timeless and spaceless realm of samadhi. This Chan master embodied the saying, "Seemingly only seven days have passed on the mountain, yet thousands of years have gone by in the world."

In the dimension of Dharmadhatu, Buddhist masters like Xu Yun are no longer confined by illusive boundaries or plagued by fluctuating emotions. Their pure and true nature spans the entire universe and they are at ease in every moment. Their Dharma body is omnipresent and always at peace. They can eat one simple meal a day and not feel hungry. They can sleep under a tree and be in bliss, never experiencing cold, discomfort, or fear. The time and space of their lives is captured in the following verse, "Mountain monks do not think much about time; a falling leaf announces that autumn has arrived." Chan

Master Lai Rong's life demonstrates this truth. He abandoned fame and fortune to become a monk. With only the bare necessities, consisting of a pair of shoes and a patched robe made out of rags, he retreated to the mountains to cultivate his wisdom and become one with the Dharma. His younger sister felt sorry for his impoverished lifestyle and took some food and clothing to the small cave that he called home. When his sister arrived, Lai Rong kept his eyes closed, did not utter a word, and continued to sit perfectly still in meditation. Seeking her brother's acknowledgment and the confirmation that he was well, she grew impatient and upset with his unresponsiveness. Consequently, she threw the things she had brought for him into the cave and left. Thirteen years went by, and his sister continued to think of him every day. Unable to stop worrying about her brother, the sister paid him another visit. He was still sitting perfectly stationary in meditation. The clothing and food she had brought thirteen years prior remained in exactly the same position, untouched, and completely covered with dust.

Chan Master Gaofeng Miao of the Yuan Dynasty also decided to retreat to a mountain cave to cultivate a higher spiritual state of being. There was originally a ladder leading up to the cave entrance. Once he entered the cave, he threw the ladder down and was determined not to leave. Many people pitied him because he could not wash his clothes, take a bath, trim his hair, shave his beard, or have anything substantial to eat. His chosen living space was so narrow that there was barely any room for him to shift positions. He did not have anyone to talk to and not a friend visited him. Yet Chan Master Gaofeng Miao endured the unendurable. He overcame the impossible and eliminated both the requirement and the desire for what we consider basic human needs. Although he did not have a change of clean clothing, his Dharma appearance was majestic. Although there was no water for bathing, his heart was pure and untainted. He could not shave his hair and beard, yet he completely eradicated his distress. He did not have any delicious food to eat, yet he savored the delight of meditation and the endless flavor of the Dharma. He received no company, but the flowers and trees of nature were full of vitality. Everything he saw was prajna; every condition he found was wondrous truth. His joy was boundless and indescribable.

The freedom and delight enjoyed by these holy practitioners in their liberated state of time and space cannot be matched in our modern materialistic society. In today's world, people mainly focus on pursuing material satisfaction and sensory pleasure. They neglect cultivating peace and serenity of the mind. In reality, the accumulation of possessions does not lead to satisfaction; material desire will only increase greed and suffering. As a result, people become trapped in the painful mire of evil and cannot break free. Ignoring our spiritual dimension is truly a pity; it shackles us to the turbulence of worldly existence. Poet Lu You of the Song Dynasty wrote the following poem to reflect this:

> My body is like a swallow, always being the guest year after year.
> My mind admires the wandering monks; for them everywhere is home.
> The breeze of spring enables me to clearly understand life
> And accompanies me as I travel throughout the world.

In this modern age, many people find themselves constantly stressed by work and depressed by life. When the days become unbearable, they go for a vacation abroad in the effort to relax and reduce their anxiety. They seek distraction and escape from the pressure and distress they feel. Some may visit Southeast Asia, Japan, or Korea. Others try to find relaxation and pleasure by traveling to European countries or Africa. Their misdirected efforts are like digging a new well each time they feel thirsty; their flawed plan ignores the importance of attaining relief without wasting effort. The temporary relief they feel can never completely liberate anyone from the confines of time and space. For the ultimate liberation, it is much better to observe and cultivate the teachings of Buddhism. Merely changing one's location and spending time away from the cause of pain does not provide true freedom; it is superficial and fleeting. The Buddhist sages can attain eternity in an instant. They can realize the endless universe in a grain of sand. The limitless Dharma and the infinite universe are already in our hearts. Why struggle to search for them outside?

Countless Chan masters have the power to penetrate time and space. By focusing on letting go, they can instantly detach themselves from everything. When free of attachments, so the saying goes, "The mind can travel into antiquity; a thought can traverse ten thousand years." They are released from the restrictions and hindrances of time and space. They are in the company of the Buddhas. Let me illustrate this point by sharing the Yunmen sect's legend of "Chan Master Ling Shu Welcoming the Head Teacher."

During the late Liang Dynasty, Chan Master Zhi Sheng (also known as Chan Master Ling Shu) taught in Ling Shu Temple, which was located near the present-day county of Qu Jiang in Guangdong province. The temple had hundreds of resident monks, yet there was not a head teacher in charge. Many monastics urged Master Zhi Sheng, "Since we have so many monks in this temple now, you should appoint a head teacher."

Master Zhi Sheng reflected for a moment, and replied, "The head teacher of this temple has already been born into this world. He is now herding sheep. We must simply be patient."

A few years went by and nothing happened. Others once again urged Master Zhi Sheng to appoint a head teacher. Master Zhi Sheng nodded, "It will be very soon. Our head teacher has already renounced household life to become a monk. Please continue to practice patience."

Many years passed, yet the position remained vacant. The monastics raised the question again, and Master Zhi Sheng, now much older, smiled and said, "The causes and conditions are gradually ripening. Our head teacher is now traveling and studying Chan under many different masters."

After many exchanges of this nature, Master Zhi Sheng still remained calm and unperturbed. Twenty-two years passed and Master Zhi Sheng was growing old. Everyone was now worried. Once more they raised the issue of the head teacher with him. Master Zhi Sheng looked up to the sky and smiled. He assured everyone, "Good! Good! Our head teacher has finally crossed the Five Mountains Range and is heading this way. We will only have to wait a short while longer."

With this comment, he retreated to his room to meditate. Looking at each other, the monks started to discuss the perplexing situation among themselves. More time passed. One day, the old master asked the disciples to clean up the vacant quarters of the head teacher. The old master even inspected the room himself. A few days later, the big bell was rung. Everyone knew it was the signal that the head teacher had finally arrived and that they should put on their formal robes. They were called to gather before the entrance to welcome the long-awaited head teacher. Everyone followed the elderly master and stood outside the monastery entrance. Soon, a monk arrived with his alms bowl.

With a smile, Master Zhi Sheng greeted the monk, "Welcome Master Yunmen Wenyan. We are joyful you have come. Our head teacher position has been vacant for several decades now. Why did you wait until today to arrive?"

Wenyan respectfully joined his palms together and replied, "Everything is determined by previous causes and conditions. The length of time and distance in space are not important. Am

I not finally here?" Master Zhi Sheng smiled with understanding. Accompanied by all the disciples, he escorted Wenyan into the main shrine and at long last formally appointed him as the head teacher.

Take a moment to pause in your reading and reflect upon these stories. How free are the lives of these Chan masters! How unconstrained is their time and space! In contrast, people of the present day feast on gourmet food but are not satisfied. They achieve fame and fortune but do not know peace. They sleep on comfortable mattresses but toss and turn all night. They reside in mansions but feel insecure. They fight and struggle against self-imposed boundaries every day. They never experience the wonder of limitless time and infinite space. A life of such small proportions is truly regrettable.

THE UTILIZATION OF TIME AND SPACE

In Buddhism, there is a saying, "The mind encompasses the space of the universe, traversing realms as numerous as all the grains of sand." This means that for those who use time and space wisely, their time is the time of the mind. They can freely journey from past to present. They have endless Chan wisdom and application. The universe is their time. Their space is the space where the Dharma flows. It freely spans all dimensions. The representation and manifestation of principles are limitless. The Dharmadhatu is their space.

Conversely, for those who do not use time and space wisely, their time is constrained by the movements of the clock, and they are controlled by the finite concepts of seconds, hours, months and years. To them, a minute is a minute, no more and no less; an hour is an hour, no more and no less. Time is finite; its use is limited. Their space is area and distance bound by feet and inches. A kilometer cannot be lengthened; a meter cannot be shortened. Their space is confined and limited.

Let me illustrate this misuse of time and space with an

example. A devotee once asked Chan Master Zhaozhou, "How can I use the twelve hours of a day wisely?"

Master Zhaozhou stared at him and responded, "You are bound by the twelve hours of the day. Your attachment controls you and prevents your wisdom from sprouting. I use my twelve hours appropriately and am not enslaved by a small perspective. What kind of time are you talking about?"

Wise people know how to use time and space perfectly; they lead free and harmonious lives. Fools are enslaved by time and space; they are busy running around all day, fretting over the passing minutes. Wise or foolish, the differences in peace of mind and depth of wisdom are obvious.

There is an ancient fable called "Marking the Boat to Recover a Sword," which illustrates what happens when one is ignorant of time and space. In the country of Chu, a man was crossing a river on a ferry. In the middle of the river, he accidentally dropped his sword into the water. Everybody urged him to dive into the water to recover the sword. He was not worried; instead, he leisurely made a mark on the boat. He was quite proud of his idea and replied confidently while pointing to his mark, "My sword fell down from here. When the boat stops, I will dive for my sword from this point. Why worry?" Others told him that because both the boat and water were moving, it would be impossible for his sword to follow the boat and remain aligned with this mark. With time passing and space changing, he surely could not retrieve his sword in this manner. He did not listen to their concerns. When the boat finally docked, he started looking for the sword beneath the mark on the boat. Do you suppose he succeeded in retrieving his sword? Of course not; it was the wrong time and space.

Everyone in society must work, but some people just want to make a lot of money at any cost. They work feverishly day and night. They scheme and cheat, using every avenue and shortcut possible to make money. They may make hundreds of thousands of dollars a year, and over the course of their lives, they may earn a few million dollars. But where is the meaning in abandoning all ideals, ethics, and happiness for the sake of money? What is the value of life? Is it truly worthwhile to throw away a precious lifetime in exchange for a few illusive pieces of crumpled paper currency? Why do we not use our valuable time to pursue the path of real fortune and happiness?

When I arrived in Taiwan over five decades ago, not only was I unable to replace my old torn clothes and shoes, I had great difficulty obtaining a pen and some paper for writing. Sometimes I endured hunger and cold for months and still could not afford to purchase these simple items. When I saw others receiving generous offerings by conducting Dharma functions or performing services, I did not feel inadequate or envious. They bought comfortable clothing and good food; I did not feel poor or deprived. In cold weather, I warmed myself under the sun. The sun was there for everyone to enjoy. It was my robe, so wonderfully warm and comforting. During the hot season, I cooled myself with the breeze. The wind was there to keep everyone cool. It was my gown, so beautifully free and flowing. I looked at trees and flowers; they were my Dharma companions. No one could deprive me of so many Dharma companions. I walked across rivers and plains, which offered limitless Dharma delight. No one could take that away from me or tell me I didn't have enough money. My Dharma joy was so fulfilling. If our minds are broad and open, we are freely given heaven and earth, the sun and moon; they are all ours. We can have all time and space. In fact, we already do, and we simply must wake up to this truth. If all you can do is complain and get depressed about poverty and obstacles, you will be poor and ill at ease in all places and at all times. Your time and space will be an endless hell and a boundless sea of suffering.

Let me share a few more stories to illustrate how we can

intelligently use our perception of time and space as our own blessings.

One day, a young person saw a very old man. He was curious and asked, "Sir, can you tell me how old you are?"

With a smile, the gentlemen replied, "Oh! I am four. I am four years old."

The young fellow was shocked. He looked carefully at the old gentleman, and exclaimed, "Oh! Sir, please do not joke with me. Your hair is so white and your beard is so long. How could you be four?"

"Yes! I am really four!" The old man then kindly explained, "In the past, I lived a befuddled life. I was selfish and preoccupied. I wasted away a great portion of my life. It wasn't until four years ago that I discovered Buddhism. Then, I learned to do good and be helpful. I learned to rid myself of greed, hatred, and ignorance. I realized that I should cultivate myself to uncover my true nature. My entire life had not been meaningful, valuable, or fulfilling until these past four years. You asked me my age. The reason I am only four is that I truly feel I have been a wise person for only these last four years."

Virtuous deeds should be done as soon as possible. People should learn the Dharma as early as possible. Consider the following question: In your brief existence in this realm of time and space, how have you been leading your life? Have you used the opportunity to do good and to seek the truth? Have you used all available time and space to benefit others and yourself?

The sutras offer the following allegory. A king had two close attendants. The king liked his attendant on the left much better than the attendant on the right. The attendant on the right was puzzled and wondered why he was not in the king's favor. He carefully monitored the other attendant's every move, and finally he discovered the reason. When the king spat, the attendant on the left would quickly wipe the spittle off the ground with his foot. Naturally, the king liked him better. With this knowledge, the right attendant planned to imitate this behavior. However, he was always a step slower than the other attendant. Finally, he devised a plan. The next time the king was ready to spit, he would jump on the opportunity. He figured that with quick anticipation, he would be able to wipe the spit right off the king's mouth before it could land on the ground. So the next time the king was ready to spit, he reacted instantly. Unfortunately, when he kicked his foot up, he knocked out the king's teeth and bloodied his mouth instead. In his frenzied haste, he had also "wiped away" any opportunities he had to gain the king's favor.

Greed and ignorance prevent us from using time and space wisely, and we often miss valuable opportunities. Only if we want to benefit others and ourselves can we exist in boundless time and space.

Once, a high official in Japan asked Chan Master Zean about the use of time. He complained, "Ah, my position as an official is such a meaningless job. Every day, people want to flatter me. After a while, all their compliments sound the same; they're so tedious. I don't enjoy hearing all the flattery. Days seem to pass by like years. I just don't know how to kill time fast enough."

The Chan master smiled and offered him these words, "This day will never return; the passing of time is precious like a treasure." Time that has passed will never return. We should treasure our time and remember that it is precious like exquisite jade.

In modern society, it is fashionable to talk about "conservation." Unfortunately, we only emphasize conserving materials or money. We do not understand that we should also conserve time and emotion. We should conserve our desires and our lives. We should be careful with every thought and deed. We should not let ourselves be indulgent or lose control. Only then can we know how to use time and space wisely, and reap their unimaginable gifts.

Chan Master Zongyan of Japan liked to take afternoon naps. It was his habit. His students once asked him why he slept so long. He replied, "In my dreams, I visit ancient scholars and masters, much like Confucius dreaming of the Duke of Zhou. The longer my dreams are, the stronger my cultivation becomes. What do you know about this practice of 'befriending ancient scholars'?"

Shortly thereafter, a few students were scolded by the same Chan master for taking long afternoon naps. The students replied, "Well, we are learning from your example. In our dreams we have gone to seek and to study with ancient masters and scholars."

"What then have you learned from them?"

"Oh, we have learned much from them! In our dreams, we asked them, 'Is our master studying with you all the time?' They all replied, 'No, we have never seen or heard of your master.'"

One must be honest about time and space, never using it to deceive others. "Day by day, time goes by; each day will never return." The arrow of time never flies backward. If we do not seize the bountiful opportunities presented to us, we will constantly limit our vast potential. There is a very well-known poem that encourages us to heed this warning:

Youth never returns; a day just has one dawn.
Work diligently now; time waits for no one.
—TAO QIAN OF THE CHU KINGDOM

In Buddhism, the "Take Heed Verse" of Samantabhadra Bodhisattva aptly describes the urgency of using our time wisely:

This day is over; life has decreased accordingly.
As a fish in dwindling water, where is the joy?

One should work diligently, as if extinguishing flames
   on one's head.
Be mindful of impermanence; do not relax your efforts.

Time and space quickly disappear. If we want to enter unrestricted time and space, if we treasure this life and its boundless potential, we should chant "O-Mi-To-Fo (Amitabha Buddha)" and learn from "Amitabha Buddha." "Amitabha" means infinite light and infinite life. Infinite light is boundless space; infinite life is endless time. If we can know time and space as boundless and limitless, then we will have risen above their illusive confinement. We will have ventured beyond the cycles of birth and death. We will have transformed ignorance into enlightenment. We will have escaped the suffering of samsara and transcended the confusion and hindrance of worldly phenomena. We will have ventured into the bright and free world of nirvana, the Pure Land of ultimate bliss.

CHAPTER THREE

THE WHEEL OF REBIRTH

Our understanding of the Buddhist perception of time and space provides us with the basis for examining another topic that is fundamental in Buddhism—rebirth. Although it is of utmost importance within Buddhist philosophy and doctrine, the truth of rebirth is rather difficult for some to accept.

When rebirth is mentioned, some people laugh or scoff at the idea. They consider believing in rebirth passé and obsolete in this technologically advanced age. Others may think that the question of rebirth is a matter for individuals to decide based on faith. After all, the issue of what happens after death seems remote to people grappling with the challenges of everyday living. The Confucian saying, "If I don't even know about living [morally], why ask about dying?" explains why some people feel the question of rebirth is not a relevant or pressing concern. However, if we were on a battlefield, where we might come face to face with death, then we would be more inclined to ponder this very important and serious question of death and rebirth with great urgency.

Sometimes we hear young people making scornful and skeptical remarks about rebirth. By not recognizing its existence, however, they are simply limiting their understanding of life and denying the opportunity to experience great meaning and freedom in it. If there were no rebirth, there would be no past lives, and moreover, there would be no future lives. Without future lives, existence would be short and meaningless. People would drift aimlessly from day to day, uncertain about the purpose of existence and forlorn that there was absolutely nothing to look forward to after this finite set of years. In contrast, those who believe in rebirth often encourage themselves when they experience tough times by saying, "Everything is going to be all right. Just wait and see how I will be doing in ten years, or even a hundred years." Even death-row inmates facing execution can confidently declare, "In twenty years, I will be back, with another chance at life." With rebirth, human existence has room to maneuver. With rebirth, unfulfilled wishes can one day materialize, and transformations that were slow to occur will beautifully unfold. With rebirth, there will always be the next "train of life" for us to board, transporting us to new destinations with fresh experiences along the way.

No phenomena in this world can escape the workings of the wheel of rebirth. It is because of the workings of rebirth that all beings are reborn into one of six blessed or suffering realms of existence. The life processes of being born and dying are examples of rebirth. Changes in nature are also manifestations of rebirth. There is the change of the four seasons. There is the time cycle of past, present, and future. There is the cycle of day and night. All of these are temporal forms of rebirth. Changes in direction and movement from one place to the next are spatial types of rebirth. In short, everything around us is the result of rebirth and is always subject to its continuous cycle. The wind blows and gathers the clouds; clouds turn into rain, which falls to the ground. The rain evaporates into the sky and becomes clouds again. This continuous process of the water cycle is a form of rebirth. When an automobile burns gasoline, it generates energy and produces carbon dioxide. The carbon dioxide is absorbed by plants. When the plants die, they decompose and, many years later, become natural oil deposits. This is yet another form of rebirth. A light can be turned on, off, and on again. This is rebirth, as well.

The wheel of rebirth is not only found in changes in the universe; it is also evident in the many changes that people experience during their lifetime, from the time of birth to the time of death. According to scientific research, there is not a single cell in the body that does not change over the course of seven years. In other words, our bodies are completely renewed every seven years. The cellular structure, perception, and cognition of all living creatures, from simple organisms to advanced humans, are constantly moving, changing, living, and dying.

This constant state of flux, renewal, and metabolic change that we experience physically (birth, old age, sickness, and death) and in our minds (the forming, existing, changing, and ceasing of thoughts) are what we call the wheel of rebirth. The wheel of rebirth is also at work in family relationships; at one time we are the children of our parents, yet at another time we become the parents of our children. The changes in our economic welfare and the ups and downs of our emotions are also examples of rebirth. Nothing escapes the infinite patterns of change and renewal that are part of the wheel of rebirth.

Of all the examples of rebirth mentioned above, the one that we must thoroughly understand in Buddhism is the wheel of rebirth within the six realms of existence. According to the Buddhist teachings, human beings are constantly going through cycles of rebirth. These cycles, and the resulting forms that are manifested, are the direct consequences of karma. Karma is the force that is created as a result of our actions, words, and thoughts. The force of karma is what perpetuates the cycle of cause and effect and gives rise to the flow of life of which different variations of life forms, such as celestial beings, humans, spirits, and animals, are part. In Buddhism, this is referred to as the "wheel of rebirth within the six realms of existence." In his piece *Inspiration to Pledge the Bodhicitta*, Master Sheng An said, "All beings and I have been trapped in the cycle of rebirth from time eternal and cannot be liberated. Heaven and earth, here and there, we live in many forms, rising and falling." Many people who remain ignorant of its truth, however, do not accept this profound and important law. It is no wonder that ancient masters would sigh and lament, "Only the sutras can reveal such truth; only the Buddha can speak and be heard on such matters."

Let me stress, rebirth is not a religious theory; nor is it an escape or a psychological comfort to turn to when the unforgiving moment of death befalls us. It is a precise science that explains our existence from the past into the future. We should develop a thorough understanding of rebirth, not because we are expected to do so in Buddhism, but because this understanding can help us examine our lives in a broader context. In the next four sections, I will discuss the following aspects of the Buddhist perspective on the cycle of rebirth: 1) the value of understanding rebirth, 2) common questions regarding rebirth, 3) evidence of rebirth, and 4) transcending rebirth.

THE VALUE OF UNDERSTANDING REBIRTH

What value does rebirth bring to our lives? What meaning does rebirth add to our existence? Through rebirth, our existence has continuity; life is no longer limited to a short span of a hundred years or so. With rebirth, life contains unlimited hope and infinite possibilities. Within the cycle of rebirth, death is not mourned as the ultimate end, but rather celebrated as the beginning of another existence. Living and dying, dying and living, existence continues uninterrupted while possibilities and potential are unbounded. This unending process can be compared to a torch. When one stick of wood is exhausted, it is replaced with another. Each stick may be different in its components, yet the flame continues to burn. Rebirth is also like an oil lamp. When one oil lamp is exhausted, another is lit. These lamps, burning one after another, serve to shatter the darkness of the world. As we go through the cycle of rebirth within the six realms, our bodies can take on many forms, such as a "Henry" or "Jane," or even a celestial being. While the forms are different, the flame of life is inextinguishable, and the lamp of wisdom never stops burning. Rebirth is what gives our existence universality; Rebirth gives our existence continuity and meaning.

Although we may say that everyone is equal under the law, some people still manage to evade the law, or interpret it in distorted ways in an attempt to satisfy their desires. In contrast, Buddhism teaches us that the cycle of rebirth treats everyone equally. Regardless of whether one is a member of the nobility or a commoner, everyone must face the cycle of rebirth. As mentioned in the chapter on "Time and Space," this concept was eloquently expressed by the poet Du Mu: "The only thing truly equal in this world is gray hair; it does not overlook the heads of the rich." Time is the most objective judge. Birth, age, sickness, and death are the most impartial jury. Cause and effect, as well as the cycle of rebirth, are not controlled by a yama (underworld) king or a god-creator. Our circumstances, whether good or bad, are determined by our past deeds and our resulting karma. Our stored karma interacts with ripened conditions and manifests in varying types of painful or blessed effects. One sutra states, "Millions of millennia may pass, but karma does not vanish. When the condition has ripened, one must bear the consequences of one's actions." Our circumstances in the cycle of rebirth within the six realms, whether we are intelligent or dull, rich or poor, young or old, are all products of our past deeds. For example, consider the child prodigy Wang Naiqing. His talent in mathematics surpasses the capabilities of many college professors and experts. His talent is not a product of this lifetime; it is the culmination of learning from previous lifetimes. This, too, is a form of rebirth. Rebirth liberates us from the hands of a divine power, for it is our own karma that controls rebirth. Heaven and gods cannot give us fortune or bring us disaster; we are our own masters. From the viewpoint of rebirth, every being is free and equal. Happiness and fortune are the products of our own choices. Misery and tragedy are also of our own creation. A creator cannot protect us from the consequences of our own crimes; similarly, gods cannot erase the benefits of our meritorious deeds. Therefore, with respect to rebirth and cause-and-effect, there is no such thing as luck. We are all the creators of our own future.

We should lead our lives like a wheel, always moving it steadily and smoothly forward. Only then can we continually refresh our lives and encounter new possibilities. Repenting of our transgressions saves us from going backwards, like a wheel out of control in reverse; with time and remorse, we can eventually make amends. Rebirth gives us unlimited hope. Although the cold winter may be long, the warm spring will one day come. Rebirth is not a word game for argument, and its influence on our lives is not simply a question of whether we believe in it or not. Even if we stubbornly refuse to believe in rebirth, it is difficult to deny that the cycle of rebirth is all around us, permeating all of existence. In all the phenomena of society, nature, the universe, and even between you and me, everything exists within the swirl of rebirth. Therefore, the wise action for us to take is to intelligently understand rebirth, to seek liberation from it, to transcend the three realms of desire, form, and formlessness, and ultimately to transform the wheel of rebirth into the Dharma wheel of Buddhas and bodhisattvas. Only then will we be elevating our wisdom.

SOME QUESTIONS REGARDING THE SUBJECT OF REBIRTH

Because rebirth has such profound meaning and is of utmost importance in our lives, it is imperative that we seek greater clarity regarding its existence, manifestation, and purpose. Although present in every aspect of phenomena, many people still have questions about the cycle of rebirth.

Is the Existence of Rebirth Good or Bad for Us?

Some people find anguish in the thought of being reborn again. To them, it is best if death is the final chapter of their lives. Buddhism, on the other hand, believes that death is not the finale but is in fact the beginning of another life, ripe with opportunities and possibilities. Our present life is only one of our many lives, and we must learn to treasure each life so that life is not wasted. With rebirth, our lives do not just end with this one; we have another chance to build a better future. Without rebirth, death is the ultimate end. Would it not be tragic if we went to our graves with our hopes and dreams unfulfilled? How can life without rebirth be considered desirable? Rebirth, in this sense, is refreshing and renewing, allowing us to continuously develop our character, benefit other beings, and move closer to the divine realm of Buddhahood.

Why Am I Not Aware of Rebirth?

One may ask, "If rebirth really exists, how is it that I cannot recall anything in my past life?" It is said in the sutras, "Humans are pitiful; a grandson marries the grandmother." Why are we so ignorant of our past lives that we could not even recognize our own grandmother? In Chinese folklore, it is said that before one is reborn, one has to drink a concoction that erases all memory of the previous life. Similarly, Plato believed that the soul, in its journey of rebirth, had to first cross an extremely hot and arid desert before finally coming to a river of cool running water. With a thirst that was simply unbearable, one drank from the river without realizing that the water would wipe out all fragments of memory from the previous life. Ancient Roman folklore had a similar story about how one's memory of a previous life is lost after rebirth.

Buddhism teaches that people lose all memory of previous lives because of the "confusion of rebirth." After one dies, one passes through the stage of "intermediate being." An intermediate being possesses all the six senses and looks like a three-foot-tall child. It has supernatural power, can go through walls, and is able to travel at an incredible speed. Nothing can stand in its way, except for a mother's womb and the Buddha's diamond throne. The intermediate being lives and dies in seven-day increments. After it dies, it can be reborn again. At most, it can live for seven seven-day periods, or a total of forty-nine days. Some may only live for two or three seven-day periods, depending on whether the strength of their karma is particularly good or evil. Based on the distinct energy of these beings' karma, they are pulled to a certain realm of existence more quickly than those with balanced karma. At the end of this intermediate period, the being will be reborn into one of the six realms. It is because of this intermediary state that we forget our previous lives, not even recalling what realms we lived in previously. Some of you may say, "How regrettable, wouldn't life be wonderful if one could have the power of knowing one's past and future lives, and be free of the confusion of rebirth?" In fact, the absence of this power means our focus can remain rooted in the present, allowing us not to dwell on past experiences, but to create better and more elevated present moments. Without the turmoil of replaying our past mistakes and hardships, how free and pleasant life is! Thus, there are rules of nature by which the universe and life operate. When everything settles into its respective place and evolves in due order, then all can be truly at ease. We may have forgotten our past lives, but with rebirth, we have a new body, with all the unpleasant experiences of the past behind us. We only have to move forward. Is this not indeed a very wonderful thing?

Do Prayers for the Deceased Have Any Impact on Their Rebirth?

Now that we know that rebirth is real, certain questions arise: Does the saying of prayers or the reciting of sutras have any impact on the rebirth of our loved ones after they pass away? Can these actions help them to become liberated from rebirth?

According to the *Ksitigarbha Sutra*, only two to three tenths of the merit from the reading of sutras is transferred to the deceased, while the remaining merit blesses the one reading the sutra. Therefore, it is best if we ourselves recite the sutras when we are alive; it is like saving for a rainy day. In this way, we do not need to impose on others to recite the sutras for us after we have passed away.

If the merit that can be transferred to the deceased is limited, how then does the reciting of sutras benefit the deceased? It can be compared to benefiting from the connection to a wealthy and famous relative. It is like the passport that one needs to take on a trip; even merit accumulated indirectly, or merit that is but a fraction of what is needed can help a deceased relative to be reborn into the land of the Buddhas. When a rock is thrown into the ocean, it quickly sinks to the bottom. If the rock is placed on a ship, however, it can arrive at the other shore safely. The heavy karma of our sins is like this rock; we can use the compassionate merit acquired from the reciting of the sutras as the ferrying vessel so that we will not be left to sink in the sea of rebirth. As another example, if a wheat field is full of healthy and strong seedlings, a couple of weeds will not have any material impact. The merit of reciting the sutra can promote the seedlings of our good karma to grow, and prevent the buried seeds of our misdeeds from germinating.

Do Fengshui[1] and Fortune-telling Have Any Impact on Rebirth?

In Chinese culture, it is common for people to hire a soothsayer to check the time and location for weddings, funerals, and special occasions. The *Fengshui* master may tell you that the alignment of your house is not right and that it may hinder the future of your descendants. The fortune-teller may tell you that the couple's horoscopes are conflicting and that they should not get married. When we have to check the calendar of the stars to pick a good day for our weddings or to consult soothsayers for a time and place to bury our loved ones, then our lives are controlled by superstition and a belief in divine power. In reality, of the many weddings that take place on auspicious days, some may end in divorce while others endure. Therefore, having a wedding ceremony on a carefully chosen day does not guarantee a happy marriage. Instead, learning to get along and being committed to one other is the foundation for a blissful and lasting union.

Actually, the foundation of so-called *Fengshui* and auspicious timing should be built on relationships and mental attitudes. If we want favorable *Fengshui* and auspicious timing, we need to direct our efforts toward helping others and toward building good affinities with others. In doing so, we will find that every place is a perfect location and any time is an auspicious moment. Accordingly, if we believe in rebirth, it makes sense that we should diligently cultivate our virtues and accumulate our merits, because our virtues and merits can be reborn with us, traveling through lifetime after lifetime. We should also form good causal relationships with others, for they, too, can be reborn with us. Indeed, accumulating merits and building good causal relationships with others instead of relying

---

1. The belief that the direction and surroundings of a house, or a tomb, can influence the fortune of a family and its offspring. Also spelled "Feng shui."

upon superstitious practices are the ultimate source of happiness in life.

Are There Any Examples That Can Illustrate the Existence of Rebirth?

Since there is no way for one to know the past and future, it is important to examine some real-life examples that substantiate the existence of rebirth. For example, ponder the silk clothing that we wear. It is made by silkworms. Silkworms spin cocoons from which silk moths emerge. Silkworms, cocoons, and moths are three entities, yet they are also one being. Therefore, it is inaccurate to say that a silkworm is *not* a silkmoth; however, it is just as inaccurate to say that a silkworm is the *same* as a silkmoth. We are just as correct to say that a silkworm *is* a silkmoth as to say that a silkworm *is not* a silkmoth. Is this example of rebirth from the natural world not transparent?

Allow me to share another story that underscores the meaning of rebirth. Once there was a man who stole some coconuts. While he was savoring the taste of the coconuts, he was caught red-handed by the owner. The owner grabbed him and yelled angrily, "How can you steal my coconuts?"

"I did *not* steal your coconuts!"

"How can you deny it? I planted the coconut tree!" the owner fumed.

Indignantly, the man argued, "Well, the coconut you planted is the seed in the ground, while I am eating the fruit on the tree. What does that have to do with you?"

Clearly, the clever thief was attempting to distort a basic process of nature and the law of rebirth. The coconuts on the tree grow out of the coconut seed in the ground; they are connected through rebirth. Like the metamorphosis of a seed into a coconut, or the seamless transformation of a silkworm, life goes on and on. The wheel of life turns and turns, without a moment of respite.

Is the Idea of Rebirth in Conflict with
the Concept of No-self?

One of the fundamental teachings of Buddhism is that "All dharmas do not have a substantial self." If this is the case, then how can rebirth exist? Are these two truths in conflict with each other? "No-self" does not mean that there is a lack of life. Rather, it means that our physical bodies are the illusive and impermanent combination of the five aggregates (form, feeling, perception, mental formation, and consciousness) and the four great elements (earth, water, fire, and wind). This combination exists provided that the right causes and conditions are present. Thus, our physical bodies do not have a substantial self; this is what is meant by no-self.

Therefore, the idea of rebirth, an embodied result of the five aggregates and four great elements, is not in conflict with the concept of no-self. Also consider the example of a piece of gold. It can be molded into rings, earrings, or bracelets. The forms may vary, yet the nature of gold is unchanged. The same is true of our existence. In a perpetual flux through the wheel of rebirth, we wander between the heaven and earth realms. We may be a "Jack" or a "Mary," a donkey or a horse. What actually travels through the wheel of rebirth is not the physical body, but rather what Buddhism calls *alaya-vijnana* (storehouse of consciousness) that is within every one of us.

What Is at the Core of Rebirth?

If it is not the physical body that is reborn, then what is this *alaya-vijnana* that is at the core of rebirth? In the sutras, this core of rebirth is described as follows: The vast Tripitaka cannot describe the *alaya-vijnana* completely. Impacted by the winds of circumstance, the seven abysmally deep waves[2] arise

---

2. The seven types of consciousness, which are sight, sound, smell, taste, touch, mental, and mano (or ego) consciousness.

from it. Through the effect of contact, it holds seeds for sense organs, entities of beings, and the physical world.[3] The first to come and the last to go, it acts as the arbiter of existence.

Alaya-vijnana is the basic source of life. As it comes into contact with different conditions and circumstances, it gives rise to various mental formations and actions, thus producing karma. The seeds of karma are in turn stored back in this giant warehouse of *alaya-vijnana*. The relative abundance of the good or bad karma in this giant warehouse then determines the direction of the next rebirth. When a being dies, the *alaya-vijnana* is the last to leave the physical body. When a being is reborn, the *alaya-vijnana* is the first to arrive in the next body. It is the core of rebirth.

What Is the Relationship between Rebirth and the Force of the Good or Bad Karma that We Have?

Given that the *alaya-vijnana* is the core of rebirth, what then determines the conditions and circumstances that direct our rebirth? Every day, we create endless karma based on our actions, words, and thoughts. Some of this karma is wholesome, while some is unwholesome. Karma derived from virtuous choices and from bad choices forms two dominating and competing forces, much like the situation in a tug-of-war. If the force of the wholesome karma dominates, we will be reborn into one of the three good realms of celestial, human, or asura existence. If the force of the unwholesome karma is stronger, we will be reborn in one of the three suffering realms of animals, hungry ghosts, or hell.

Thus it is the relative quality of karma that decides the future of our rebirths. From this, we can conclude that if we want to prepare for our future well-being, it is critical that we do good and refrain from evil.

---

3. Refers to the world that constitutes the living environment of living beings.

What Do Different Religions Say Is the Final Goal of Rebirth?

Almost all religions accept the idea of rebirth, but their beliefs vary regarding its ultimate goal. Daoists seek everlasting life and permanent youth. Christians believe that the final goal is to enter into heaven, to be with God, and to achieve eternal salvation. Even most folk religions espouse everlasting life. These philosophies are different from the Buddhist perspective, which sees the ultimate goal of rebirth as realizing the state of non-arising. This goal instructs us to strive toward complete liberation from the cycle of rebirth through spiritual cultivation and righteous living. From a Buddhist perspective, an everlasting, cyclical lifetime would keep us trapped in the agony of rebirth. Only non-arising can emancipate us from the suffering of existence. It is the ultimately serene, eternally joyous, and absolutely pure state of existence!

EVIDENCE OF REBIRTH

There are many well-documented records of famous scholars that will substantiate the truth of rebirth.

Wang Yangming, a famous Confucian scholar of the Ming Dynasty, once visited the Gold Mountain Temple to pay his respects. While at the temple, he had a feeling of *déjà vu*, as if he had been there before. As he toured the temple, he came across a room with a door that was locked and sealed. He experienced a distinct sensation that he had lived in that room before. The strength of this feeling and his rising curiosity finally compelled him to ask the receiving monk to show him the inside of the room. The monk replied apologetically, "I am very sorry. This room is where one of our founding masters passed away over fifty years ago, and his body is still kept inside. He left instructions that this room was not to be disturbed. I hope you can understand why we absolutely cannot unseal the door."

"Since the room has a door, it cannot simply remain shut

forever. Please kindly indulge me and let me go inside to take a look."

After repeated pleadings from Wang Yangming, the monk realized that this guest would not leave unless he was allowed to see the inside of the room. So the monk finally opened the door and let him in. In the dim light of dusk, he saw an old monk, who had long since passed away, sitting up straight on a mat. When he took a closer look, he was shocked! How could the face of this master look so much like his own? He glanced around the room and discovered a poem written on the wall. It went as follows:

> Wang Yangming, fifty years later,
> The person who opens the door is the one who closed it.
> When the consciousness that once left returns,
> It then believes in the Chan teaching of the indestructible
> being.

You may have already correctly assumed that the deceased monk was none other than Wang Yangming in his previous life. Having closed the door fifty years ago, he once again returned to open it. In that very moment, Wang Yangming glimpsed the truth of rebirth. As a testimonial for future generations, he wrote the following poem:

> The Gold Mountain awakened me like the strike of a fist;
> I see through the sky under Weiyang Lake.
> While enjoying the moon above the balcony,
> The playing of the flute awakens the dragon within me.

Among the public records of Xiushiu County of Jiangxi Province is the report of a woman reborn as a renowned scholar named Huang Shangu. He became a county commissioner at the tender age of twenty-five. On his twenty-sixth birthday, he dreamed that he had walked into a strange place. There, he saw a silver-haired old woman preparing and making offerings in front of her residence. On her altar was a bowl of noodles and celery. The bowl of noodles smelled so appetizing that, without any hesitation, Huang Shangu picked up the bowl from the altar and began eating. When he woke up, he could still taste the celery in his mouth. Despite the evidence, Huang Shangu still thought it was all just a dream and did not think much more about it. The next day, however, when he took an afternoon nap, he had the same dream again. He became very unsettled and decided to see if he could find the place he had envisioned in the dream. After walking quite a distance, he came upon a house in front of which was the same old woman from his dream. She was praying quietly, holding three sticks of incense in her hands. Even more incredible was the freshly prepared bowl of noodles and celery on her altar. As in the dream, the lovingly prepared food smelled delicious. Huang Shangu was very curious, so he approached the woman and asked her, "Madam! What are you doing?"

"Yesterday was the twenty-sixth anniversary of my daughter's passing. I am making an offering to her."

Huang Shangu was taken by surprise to hear that the twenty-sixth anniversary of his birth was also the twenty-sixth anniversary of this young woman's death. So he asked further, "What did your daughter usually like to do?"

"When she was alive, she was a devoted Buddhist and liked to read Buddhist sutras. She vowed not to get married and was especially fond of noodles and celery. Therefore, I prepared a special bowl of noodles and celery to offer her."

With many unanswered questions in his mind, and a growing sense of familiarity, he asked, "Would it be possible for me to look around her room?"

The woman agreed and showed him inside. The room was full of many books and sutras that he had once read. In the cor-

ner, there was a giant chest that drew Huang Shangu's attention. "What is inside this chest?" he asked. "May I open it and
take a look?"

The woman replied that she did not know what was inside
the chest or even where the key was. Huang Shangu thought
hard for a moment. Then, as if suddenly remembering something, he quickly found the key and opened the chest. He was
dumbfounded when he realized that the chest was full of his
essays and writings from each of the prior government exami-
nations he had taken only a few years earlier. He finally realized that the lonely, elderly woman had been his mother in a
previous life. He fell to his knees and pleaded, "Madam! *I was
your daughter.* Please come home with me and allow me to
take good care of you."

He then welcomed the old woman into his home and wrote
a poem to mark this amazing discovery.

> Like a monk with hair, like a layman free of worldly dust,
> Having a dream within a dream, I see existence beyond exis-
> tence.

The meaning of this poem is as follows: although he was a
layman, he aspired to the life of a monk; although he led a secular life, he was not hindered by worldly temptations. Life is like
a dream; beyond life there is another existence. This story evokes
the saying, "In dreams, vivid are the six realms of existence.
Upon awakening, empty is the universe without substance."

There is also a well-known story regarding the rebirth of the
Fifth Patriarch of the Chan school, Hong Ren. It is said that
Hong Ren was an old gardener in his previous life. He had a
very high regard for the Fourth Patriarch, Dao Xin, and wanted to become his disciple. Dao Xin thought that he was too old
and would not be able to sustain the rigors of travel necessary
to propagate the Dharma. He therefore consoled the old gar-

dener, "If you were to be reborn now, I might be able to stay on a few years longer to wait for you and teach you."

The old gardener bid the Fourth Patriarch farewell. He went by a creek and saw a young woman washing cotton yarn. Without knowing why, he asked her, "Miss, may I stay in your house for a while?"

"You should ask my parents. I cannot make such a decision."

"I must have your permission, otherwise, I will not dare to ask further."

When the young woman noticed that it was becoming dark and that the poor old man needed shelter for the night, she nodded her consent. Strangely, upon returning home, this unwed woman was suddenly pregnant. The family was very upset and disowned her. She later gave birth to a fair and healthy baby boy. She was alone and distraught and threw her ill-fated baby boy in the river. Instead of drowning, however, the baby miraculously floated upstream against the strong current. Seeing that her desperate plan had failed, she retrieved her son, who appeared unfazed. Without any means of livelihood, the young woman became a beggar to support herself and the baby. Since no one knew who his father was, he was called the "Nameless Kid." Six years went by and the baby grew to become a very lovable and intelligent young boy. One day, when Master Dao Xin was teaching in the area, the young boy went up to him, tugged at the Master's robe, and would not let go. He earnestly asked the master to take him as a disciple. When the Master saw that he was only a young boy, he patted the youngster on the head and said gently, "You are too young. How can you renounce your household life and become my disciple?"

But the "Nameless Kid," as if fully grown, demanded an answer: "Master, you complained that I was too old in the past; now you say I am too young. When are you going to accept me as your disciple?"

These words seemed to stir something deep in Master Dao Xin's memory. He quickly asked, "Child, what is your name? Where do you live?"

"They call me the 'Nameless Kid.' I live on Ten Mile Lane."

"Everyone has a name. How can you lie and say that you have no name? Please, tell me your family name."

"Buddha Nature is my family name, so I do not have a last name."

Dao Xin was very pleased that a young child could have spoken such impressive words and possessed such profound wisdom. The Master believed that this young child would one day achieve greatness and make significant contributions to Buddhism. Later, the Fourth Patriarch ceremoniously passed his robe and bowl to the "Nameless Kid," who then became the Fifth Patriarch of the Chan school. The Fifth Patriarch had many disciples, and the Chan school truly blossomed under his guidance.

In 1942, in the Pin County of Shanxi Province in China, there lived a man named Tian Sanniu. He made his home in a cave. During a storm, the cave collapsed and buried him alive. Though suffocating and helpless, he felt himself climbing out of the mound of dirt that covered him. When he emerged from the pile of earth, he saw his family huddled together, crying. He asked them what had happened, but no one acknowledged his presence. Annoyed and irritated, he walked away from his family and found himself at Mingyu Pond. There he saw a narrow door, so he decided to squeeze through the small opening. Suddenly, in the midst of many voices, he heard someone remark, "Congratulations! You have a new son."

Unknowingly, Tian Sanniu was reborn as a son of the Zhang family; he was named Zhang Shengyou. As soon as he came out of his mother's womb, he observed that the midwife was having trouble finding a pair of scissors. He asked her, "Isn't the pair of scissors hanging on the wall?"

Everyone in the room was speechless. How could an infant possibly speak? They thought that he was some sort of demon and suggested that they drown him in the river. Thankfully, his mother objected to this cruelty because she felt sorry for him, and he was spared. For seven years, he did not dare to speak a single word, yet he remembered everything of his past life. Somehow the news of Tian Sanniu's rebirth as the son of the Zhang family reached the Tian family. Just around this time, the Tian family was having a land dispute with their neighbor, but they could not find the deed to the land to prove ownership. In desperation, they asked the Zhangs' son to come to their house to look for the deed. Amazingly, the young boy was very familiar with the affairs of the family. He located the deed in no time and thereby resolved the argument.

Su Dongpo, the famous Chinese poet, gives us yet another incredible account of rebirth. He always had a deep relationship with Buddhism and was very close to a few monks, calling on them often. In the *Record of the Transmission of the Lamp for the Laity*, it was documented that the poet was the Precept Master of the Fifth Patriarch of the Chan school in his previous life. When his mother was pregnant with him, she dreamed of a thin, elderly small-eyed monk. She later gave birth to Su Dongpo. Many years later, through his brother, Su Zhe, who was a government official in Kaoan, Su Dongpo became friends with three monks, Zheng Jing, Wen Sheng, and Shou Chong. They often met to discuss Chan and the Dharma. One day, the three monks all dreamed of a visit from the deceased Precept Master of the Fifth Patriarch. Precisely at the moment when they were discussing the dream, Su Dongpo arrived for a visit. They told Su Dongpo their dream. In response, Su Dongpo told them that when he was about seven, he dreamed of himself as a monk traveling and spreading the Buddhist teachings in the Shanyou area.

Master Zheng Jing immediately added, "The Precept Master

was also from the Shanyou area. He traveled to Kaoan in his twilight years and passed away fifty years ago in Dayu." Pursuing the striking coincidences further, they found that Su Dongpo was forty-nine years old. It then dawned on all of them that Su Dongpo had been the Precept Master in his previous life.

Su Dongpo is the author of a book that contains a moving story of rebirth related to a famous Chinese proverb. The verse honors and signifies the depth and extent of a relationship, saying, "A relationship is destined to last three lifetimes." The story, in his book titled *The Legend of Monk Yuanzhe*, describes a friendship between Chan Master Yuanzhe and scholar Li Yuan. Both of them had planned to travel to Ermei Mountain together, but they could not agree upon which route to take. Yuanzhe wanted to travel by land, but Li Yuan insisted on going by river. Master Yuanzhe sighed, "Everything is determined by causes and conditions, not by the wish of a person." After examining their circumstances, they finally decided to take the water route. While passing by Nanpu, they saw a pregnant woman fetching water with a jug along the river. Yuanzhe heaved a long sigh and said, "It is precisely because I was afraid to run into this woman that I suggested taking the land route. She is from the Wang family, and I am supposed to be her son. For three years, I have been hiding from her. Consequently, she has been pregnant for three years and cannot give birth. In three days, you can go over to her house to visit me. I will acknowledge you with a smile. In thirteen years, we can meet again outside the Tianzhu temple in Hangzhou."

That evening, Master Yuanzhe passed away painlessly. Three days later, as instructed, Yuan Li paid a visit to the woman's house. The newborn baby indeed gave Yuan Li a very warm and knowing smile upon seeing him. Thirteen years later, Yuan Li traveled to the Tianzhu temple. There, he saw a young herder riding and singing on top of an ox:

An ancient apparition sits atop the boulder of the past,
   present, and future,
Enjoying the scenery and not wanting to argue.
I am happy a sentimental friend has come to visit from afar.
This body is different, but the nature is eternally the same.

When Yuan Li heard the song, he called out, "How is Chan Master Yuanzhe doing?"

The young herder waved backed and replied, "Mr. Li indeed keeps his promise." He kept playing his flute and slowly rode off into the horizon.

How We Can Transcend Rebirth

Now that we have completed a thorough examination of the existence, significance, and veracity of rebirth, we should proceed further and discover how we can transcend it. Achieving a clear understanding of rebirth is only a process, a means to reach the ultimate end of transcending rebirth.

Some people find the Buddhist tenet regarding rebirth superstitious and ludicrous. In actuality, all of the Buddha's teachings are nothing more than practical methods for liberating ourselves from the shackles of rebirth. All sutras, chants, precepts, and other forms of practice guide us toward true freedom from the churning of this perpetual cycle. Since the ultimate purpose of Buddhism is to transcend rebirth, Buddhism is indeed a sensible and rational religion that can shatter the wheel of rebirth. It is through immersion in the teachings that we find helpful tools and skillful means for ultimate liberation and transcendence.

If we want to transcend rebirth, we must first know the reason for rebirth. We are trapped in the cycle of rebirth due to our tendency to grasp and cling to worldly phenomena and perceived limits, while the circumstance of our rebirth is determined by the nature of our karma. Since the karmic forces within each of us may be wholesome or unwholesome, mild or severe, their respective effects and results are also different. It is written in the sutras, "Cutting down a tree without taking out the root, the tree will grow once more. Severing only our desires without eradicating the root causes will lead us to repeatedly experience the pain of rebirth. Such superficial transformation is like making an arrow and striking oneself with it. The sharp arrow of physical cravings also leaves us spinning in constant motion, and the arrow of desire is the same; its piercing blade hurts all beings." The thirst and craving of our greed and desires is the arrow. This arrow causes us to float and sink without ceasing in the sea of rebirth. How painful! We must apply the fire of diligence to incinerate the forest of desires. We must use the radiance of prajna-wisdom to pierce through the darkness of ignorance and unwholesome karma. We must wield the sword of wisdom to sever the chains of rebirth. With diligence and prajna-wisdom, we have great hope and powerful guidance. The Buddha once said, "This is my last rebirth." With the eighty-four thousand Dharma methods the Buddha has taught us, we can all surely break through the wheel of rebirth and live in the realm of total freedom.

After understanding rebirth, and thereby achieving liberation from its grip, the next step is not to be afraid of rebirth. This next level is ultimate transcendence that allows us to live in rebirth and not suffer in it or be corrupted by it. Unenlightened beings are led by the force of their karma into rebirth; sravakas and pratyeka-buddhas attain liberation from rebirth but remain on this plane removed from humanity, without dedicating their lives to benefit others. In contrast, bodhisattvas make great vows and pledge to be reborn to help others; this act demonstrates ultimate transcendence. Because the altruistic choice of being reborn is made through their own will, not through the directing force of karma, bodhisattvas are free from suffering when they are reborn.

Avalokitesvara Bodhisattva is one such example. This Bodhisattva steers the vessel of compassion in order to re-enter the world to deliver all beings. Similarly, Venerable Ci Hang promised to return at a certain time for the purpose of benefiting others. In the *Annals of Pure Land Holy Practitioners*, it is recorded that many masters wish to be reborn in the Pure Land so they may come back to our world in order to help others. Many Tibetan lamas are reborn into this world after passing away. The Dalai Lama and the Panchen Lama are some of the better-known examples. These masters truly live in accordance with the Bodhisattva's vow of compassion. Their generous spirit is captured in the saying, "We wish for the liberation of all beings from pain and will not seek comfort only for ourselves." They are not deserters of humanity; they are perfectly willing to be lifeboats in the sea of misery. They can be compared to lotus blossoms that sprout out of the mud, yet remain pure. They are reborn into this suffering saha world, yet are free of the pain of rebirth; they have risen above its agony. They choose to re-enter the wheel of rebirth without any hesitation, and they are not afflicted by the sufferings of rebirth. They are truly masters who have transcended the wheel of rebirth.

Indeed, we can also look into the Jataka[4] tales of the Buddha to find that the Buddha himself had been reborn as a deity, an animal, a monk, and as royalty. Without shying away from the cycle of rebirth, the Buddha diligently practiced the way of compassion and wisdom, always striving to deliver all sentient beings and manifesting the bodhi path.

When the founder of the Wei Yang school, Chan Master Weishan Lingyou, was about to pass away, his disciples gathered around him and asked, "Master, with your level of cultivation, where are you going to be reborn after passing away?"

"Oh! I will be reborn as a water buffalo at a nearby farm."

---

4. The sutra containing stories of the Buddha's past lives and his practice therein.

His disciples were shocked and puzzled, so they asked, "Master, you are such a great practitioner. How can you possibly be reborn as an animal?"

"If you do not believe me, you can find the words 'Weishan Lingyou monk' under the buffalo's left front leg. You will then know that it is me."

His disciples were grief-stricken by his passing. After the funeral, they searched for a buffalo calf and soon found a newborn on a farm nearby. They quickly looked at the creature's left front leg and indeed discovered their master's name. When they saw the buffalo toiling under the blazing sun, they could not bear the thought of their previous master suffering. They immediately bought the buffalo so they could tenderly care for it in the temple. Every morning they fed him fresh green grass. But to their dismay, the buffalo refused to eat or drink. Helpless, they took the buffalo back to the farm. There, the buffalo worked hard and then happily chewed on its hay.

Master Weishan Lingyou's humble compassion illustrates the saying, "If one wishes to become a great sage of Buddhism, one must first be willing to be a servant of all beings." His rebirth into the animal realm was not a karmic result but a selfless and benevolent condition of his own choosing. This supreme level of compassion was beyond the shallow understanding of his disciples. It is only when one is able to practice the Buddhist teachings amid the sea of rebirth and be at ease within the bounds of reincarnation that one truly understands rebirth. Such a cultivator is a bodhisattva who has truly transcended rebirth.

This chapter has outlined the Buddhist perspective on the wheel of rebirth. My main goal is to help all of us face life and the future with confidence and radiance. We must believe in the opportunity for renewal. Death is like the disintegration of a dilapidated house; we must simply move to another comfortable and sturdy house. Death is like the fraying of worn clothing; we must simply change into beautiful, new attire. In the constant flux of life, all of us should first work to complete the majestic temple within us; we should work to weave the magnificent Dharma robe within us, so that we may all be liberated from and transcend rebirth, attaining lives of bodhi wisdom even within the endless swirl of existence.

CHAPTER FOUR

SUPERNATURAL POWERS

As with the question of rebirth, the Buddhist perspective on supernatural powers can often intrigue and even baffle the Western mind. In this chapter, I will show that the Buddhist perspective is not based on superstition or mysticism. Instead, it is perfectly consistent with Buddhism's rational and practical understanding of rebirth and karma. With this fundamental distinction in mind, I will explore concepts and manifestations of magic and the supernatural by examining various definitions and classifications of magic. I will also address in this chapter magic in different social contexts, the cultivation and use of magic, and, lastly, specific teachings within the Buddhist tradition that illustrate the many forms, purposes and possibilities of magic.

When the word "magic" is mentioned, we immediately think of mysterious and unusual occurrences and superhuman actions. When we face an obstacle or tragedy, don't we all wish for a miracle? Maybe a superhero will appear and eliminate our problems. When someone hits or curses us, wouldn't it be perfect if we were martial arts masters? We could use one little finger to pin him or her to the ground. When being chased, wouldn't it be wonderful if we could fly? When someone wants to cause trouble, wouldn't it be nice if we could whisper a spell to paralyze that person? When a rich person does not believe in doing good, wouldn't it be delightful if we could magically gather his or her money and give it to the poor and needy? Magic, to most people, is essentially the wish to be outstanding, to be powerful, and to be capable of accomplishing what appears to be impossible.

Although magic can be used to punish evil and propagate goodness, it can also be misused, causing danger and harm to humanity. Magic has such disparate capabilities, compelling us to ask questions such as: Is magic good or bad, or both? What is the meaning of its existence? Does magic have any benefit for society? In this chapter, I discuss the answers to these questions from the Buddhist perspective on magic and the supernatural.

DEFINITIONS AND CLASSIFICATIONS
OF SUPERNATURAL POWERS

According to sacred Buddhist scriptures, magic is a supernormal, unlimited, unimaginable power that can be attained through the deepest meditation practice. We often believe that only Buddhas, bodhisattvas, gods, and fairies have magical or supernatural power. In actuality, ghosts and demons can also have magical power. Human beings have magical power, too. Magic is not limited to the unusual acts of causing rain and storms or riding on clouds; rather, magic is everywhere in our lives, and we can recognize it if we look carefully. When we are exhausted and thirsty after a long journey, a glass of water can quench our thirst. Is that glass of water not like a magic potion? A non-swimmer sinks like a rock after falling into water despite frantic yet fruitless struggles. In comparison, a good swimmer simply takes a few easy strokes and kicks in order to move around with the grace of a fish. Is this not miraculous? Beginning cyclists may grip the handlebars with all their might and still fall off their bicycles. However, expert cyclists can relinquish their grip and still remain secure on their fast-moving bicycles. Does this not seem supernatural? We can also describe amazing circus performances as magic.

The body itself is a miracle. Tears flow when one is sad, and laughter comes when one is happy. Hunger can be cured with food. Clothing can alleviate a chill. Are all these phenomena not magical? A woman's mammary glands not only secrete milk, but also vary the nutrient composition and amount according to the changing needs of the baby. Once the baby stops nursing, the mother's milk production stops automatically. Is this not amazing?

Clearly, magic is not limited to tricks and sorcery; it is everywhere. The turning of the four seasons, the blooming and wilting of flowers, the changing faces of the moon, the strange and wonderful forms of animals, are they not all manifestations of magical wonders? Magic is all around us. Aside from the ubiquitous presence of magic in nature, in some rare cases, Buddhist practitioners of deep cultivation may also acquire certain magical powers. Their profound cultivation of the Dharma or highly rigorous meditation practice can empower them to comprehend the physical laws of the universe in ways that are beyond our normal comprehension.

How many types of magical powers are recorded in the Buddhist scriptures? According to the most common classification, there are six main categories. These are: 1) celestial vision, 2) celestial hearing, 3) the power of knowing others' minds, 4) the power of performing miracles, 5) the power of knowing past lives, and 6) the power of eradicating all defilement.

Celestial Vision

Human eyes can only see large items with distinction and clarity. To examine small objects, we need a magnifying lens or microscope. Those with celestial vision, on the other hand, can detect the most minute things with ease. Human eyes can only see nearby objects, while distant objects appear blurred and indistinguishable. In contrast, people with celestial vision view faraway objects as clearly as those that are near. Our human vision is bound by our immediate surroundings. Those with celestial vision, however, can overcome any obstruction and see through walls, mountains, and other barriers, due to a deeper understanding of the underlying reality of things. Human eyes can only see in the presence of light. Celestial vision functions even in total darkness. Human vision is limited to this world. Celestial vision extends to all realms. In short, celestial vision is free and unbounded.

Celestial Hearing

Human ears hear at close range. We need amplifiers and microphones to help us hear sounds from afar. In contrast, those with celestial hearing can hear sounds clearly regardless of the distance. Maudgalyayana, the foremost in supernatural power among all the Buddha's disciples, once tried to see how far the Buddha's voice could travel. With magical power, he traveled to another Buddha world trillions of light years away. There, he used celestial hearing and discovered he could still clearly hear the Buddha's voice teaching.

We may know English or Chinese, but not Korean, Japanese, or other languages. People with linguistic talents may be able to speak many languages, but still have limited or no understanding of others. Those with celestial hearing, however, can understand all languages. In addition to complete comprehension of human languages, they also understand the singing of birds and the howling of animals.

Knowing Others' Minds

The power to know others' minds is the ability to know precisely what others are thinking. We often complain, "You just don't understand me." Certainly, it is difficult to understand ourselves, not to mention trying to understand others. However, one with the power of knowing others' minds can see the good and evil thoughts in others' minds as if looking through a clear lens. Not a single thought can escape detection.

Performing Miracles

Those with the power to perform miracles can transcend boundaries and defy constraining limitations. They can transform a single entity into an infinite multitude, and combine the infinitely many into one. For these individuals, distance is never an issue, since they can go as far as they like without hindrances. They can also move unscathed through fire or water, and travel through the ground with ease. They may choose to become invisible or to reappear. The power of performing miracles allows one to transcend the limitations of space. This power even allows people to exercise control over the sun and the moon, and to alter their surroundings at will. Performing miracles is the magical power that exempts the body from physical limitations.

Knowing Past Lives

We sometimes are so forgetful that we struggle to remember yesterday's events. Even people with excellent memory can only recall events of months or years past. However, those with the power of knowing past lives can remember events from their previous lives as clearly as if they occurred only a moment ago. Besides possessing clear vision about their own prior experiences, they know the past of other sentient beings as well. When someone dies, those with this power can also foretell the person's future retribution from karma, as well as his or her place of rebirth.

Eradicating All Defilement

Defilement—the myriad ways we dishonor our purity—is affliction. Those with the power to eradicate all defilement will no longer suffer any affliction. They will not be subjected to the cycles of birth and death, nor will they ever have to be reborn again in this world of ignorance. The first five magical powers accessible to Buddhist practitioners are useful methods of propagating spiritual development, yet ultimately they still cannot enable sentient beings to escape the rounds of rebirth. The five magical powers are therefore not the ultimate. Only the ultimate power of eradicating all defilement can deliver one beyond the cycles of rebirth.

It is critical to understand that the magic of ultimate liberation from defilement cannot be summoned easily. This level of power is one that is attained through great effort; it is not merely a supernatural skill utilized to accomplish great and necessary things. The magic resides in highly cultivated spiritual practice in which one is truly integrated with the truth of the teachings.

In addition to the classification of the six magical powers mentioned above, the sutras also distinguish between different levels of magical power according to how the power is acquired. In *Da Sheng Yi Zhang* (*The Essays on Mahayana Meanings*), magical powers are divided into those attained through four means: cultivation, meditation, casting spells, or evil spirits. According to *Zhong Jing Lu* (*Records from the Lineage Mirror*), in addition to these four methods, magic can be also obtained through karma. Allow me to elaborate on each form of acquisition.

Magic through Cultivation

The ultimate magical power is attained through devoted spiritual practice that cultivates the Middle Way. When one is enlightened to the truth of the Middle Way in all existence, one can maintain the mind without experiencing a rapid and constant rise and fall of thoughts, or creating subjective distinctions between the myriad objects and events encountered throughout the day. One intimately knows all phenomena in the universe, yet one is not attached. Power obtained through cultivation allows one to be totally liberated and free from the cycles of rebirth and the affliction of defilement.

Magic through Meditation

Magical power can also be obtained through practicing meditation. Like arhats, one can attain power through the four dhyana states and eight mental concentration levels achieved through focused meditation. Through this practice, one can understand worldly phenomena and gain unlimited knowledge of past and future lives.

Magic through Spells

Spells and potions can produce magic. These methods of obtaining magical powers are used by sorcerers and witches who call upon winds and fires and make themselves invisible by hiding under water or in the ground. This type of power is the most prone to be abused and used as a means to harm others.

Magic of Spirits

Spirits and genies can magically absorb cosmic energies from heaven and earth. After a long period of time, these spirits can manifest in human form and cause unusual and disorienting events to unfold in the human experience.

Magic as the Result of Karma

Some living beings may have magical power as the result of their karma. Beings reborn in ghostly realms can transport themselves across physical barriers and travel rapidly over long distances. Birds can fly in the sky and fish can live in the water. Different living beings experience their own unique karma that is not shared by others. The result is a colorful combination of creatures with diverse appearances and abilities.

Among the different magical powers, some are wholesome by nature and generate goodness. Other magical powers are unwholesome and can cause terrible harm. There is also great variation in the levels of influence, strength, and duration of impact when magic is employed. What we should aim for is the ultimate power of eradicating all defilement through the cultivation of wisdom. If we attain wholesome magical power through cultivation, we will be able to endure the birth and death process without being affected by the usual afflictions associated with this cycle. We will dwell in the freedom and serenity of nirvana without being attached to its comfort. We will stay away from extremes and peacefully walk the Middle Way of Buddhahood.

SUPERNATURAL POWERS IN THE SOCIAL CONTEXT

Most people in our society are particularly attracted to strange and unusual phenomena. By comparison, the profound, wonderful, and practical teachings of the Buddha do not attract the same magnitude of attention and awe. Magic does indeed have great power to intrigue large numbers of people, because it satisfies their curiosity and desire for an extraordinary and life-changing experience. What then is the relationship between magic and people's lives?

Magic Is Hope in Times of Trouble

There is a popular saying; "Every household has Amitabha. Every family has Guanyin (Avalokitesvara)." Avalokitesvara Bodhisattva is a very popular figure of devotion among Buddhist practitioners. How does Avalokitesvara Bodhisattva influence the lives of so many people? According to the "Universal Gateway" chapter of the *Lotus Sutra*, when sentient beings encounter difficulties, such as the seven calamities—including floods, fires, violence, war, etc.—Avalokitesvara Bodhisattva will protect and guide them. Sometimes this

Bodhisattva even points out a way for us to solve those seemingly impossible problems through our dreams. This Bodhisattva has boundless magical power and uses it to deliver sentient beings from suffering and tragedy. Avalokitesvara Bodhisattva thus becomes the torch of hope for helpless and miserable beings.

In addition to Avalokitesvara Bodhisattva, the goddess Mazhu is also held in high esteem for her magical powers. Because Taiwan is an island surrounded by open sea, people must live very close to these vast waters and endure unpredictable and potentially devastating dangers. Believed to protect people from drowning, Mazhu has been revered as the seafarers' guardian. Jigong, regarded as a living Buddha by many, is another popular figure of worship, because it is believed that he frequently uses magic to solve the problems of suffering people.

Another prominent example is a Buddhist monk of recent times, Venerable Miao Shan. The public regarded him as the "Living Buddha of the Golden Mountain." His life was full of unusual, colorful, and magical events. Once a young woman contracted an unusual, intractable illness and could not swallow. Eventually she went to Golden Mountain Temple for help. Venerable Miao Shan, the "Living Buddha," asked her to open her mouth and removed some mucus, and she was instantaneously and miraculously cured.

Venerable Miao Shan and the Abbot of Golden Mountain Temple, Venerable Tai Zang, were good friends. On one occasion, these two confidants were both using the communal bathing facility. Venerable Tai Zang had heard the many stories of how the "Living Buddha" had cured others and implored him, "Living Buddha, with your compassion, please cure my mother's terminal stomach disease." Immediately, the "Living Buddha" scooped up some bath water and said, "Here, this is a bowl of the soup of prajna (transcendental wisdom). Give it to your mother and she will be cured of all illness." Venerable

Tai Zang understandably hesitated, yet he could not openly protest. He thought to himself, "This has to be a joke. How can a person drink used bath water from the communal bathing facility?" Venerable Miao Shan then said, "This is why I advise you not to come to me with your illness. I have prescribed the soup of prajna, yet you treat it as used bath water. What am I supposed to do?"

Sometimes, despite numerous confirmations of a being's magical powers and obvious goodness, we distrust the unusual methods and refuse to accept the miracle. With proper awareness, cultivation, and wisdom, we need not fear what appears to be unsound or irrational.

To this date, the "Living Buddha" is still remembered and revered by many people because he could solve their problems and bring them hope. We must understand, however, that magic is not for trivial situations and is not suitable for frequent usage. However, the rare and wise use of magic is like emergency treatment: useful for expedient healing or immediate transformation in times of suffering. Just like rain during prolonged drought, magic can bring people hope in a hopeless situation.

Magic Is the Savior during Upheaval

There is a saying: "Unusual times require unusual methods." In times of upheaval, social chaos, and war, the results of teaching the Buddhist teachings may not appear with the urgency needed to ameliorate a negative situation. In such severe circumstances, magic may be employed for more immediate impact. As with a severe illness or injury, the patient must first be saved by emergency procedures and then cared for with long-term rehabilitation and treatment.

During the period of upheaval of the Five Nomadic Tribes and Sixteen States (304–439 CE), the ruthless generals Shi Le and Shi Hu led a murderous rebellion. Countless innocent lives were lost. Venerable Buddhacinga traveled from Central Asia hoping to convert the warring generals and amend the tragic situation.

"You should be kindhearted. You should care for each person and each family. Do not kill these innocent people," the Master taught the warlords.

The warlords retorted slyly, "You want us to be kindhearted. We want to see what your kind heart looks like."

"Fine. Please take a close look at it," Venerable Buddhacinga replied. He drew a sword from a nearby soldier and cut his own chest open. He took out his beating heart and spoke a few words over a basin of clean water. A white lotus miraculously blossomed out of the water. Buddhacinga then calmly handed over his heart to the warlords and said, "This is my heart, as pure as this white lotus blossom."

Such bravery and power impressed the murderous and hardened generals. They became the master's disciples, giving up their treacherous ways and vowing to learn and practice the Buddhist teachings. Buddhacinga had used magic to convert the warlords, and as a result saved millions of lives. Buddhacinga's deed demonstrates that during upheaval, magic can provide the power of a savior. The magical act served as an expedient method of altering a desperate situation, but certainly it was not Buddhacinga's magic that made the generals follow the Middle Way for the remainder of their lives. Magic is temporary; discipleship is personal devotion and a lifelong commitment.

During the Tang Dynasty, Chan Master Venerable Yin Feng also had great magical power according to the legends. Once he came across a fierce battle between two armies and tried to make peace through patient persuasion. Nobody heeded his advice. As a last resort, he threw his staff into the sky. He then flew up and danced with his staff. The battling soldiers were so awestruck by the extraordinary sight that they stopped fighting. An otherwise bloody battle was instantaneously ended by the Chan master's magic. After that event, people called him the Master of the Flying Staff.

The examples mentioned above illustrate that magic can be a great tool at times of upheaval. Some of you may think, "Great! I'll practice diligently and acquire supernatural power, too. I'll be able to capture the leaders of our enemies, and all of our problems will be solved." However, magic is not the exclusive solution to conflict; there is more to it than that. When one leader falls, there will be another, and another after that. Magic cannot solve problems completely; it can instantaneously bring resolution and healing, but it is not magic that inspires goodness to persevere. Only morality and compassion can bring everlasting peace.

During the Three Kingdoms Period (222–265 CE), the wise Zhuge Liang captured and released the rebel Meng Huo seven times. He engaged in this seemingly odd behavior because he understood that people could only be truly transformed through virtue, not with tricks or force. We need to have strong confidence in morality and compassion, even though the effects are not immediately visible. Morality and compassion will change evil habits and purify people's minds. Magic, no matter how powerful, can be used only in an emergency and only for temporary relief. People may be converted to Buddhism through a magical performance, but their lasting cultivation cannot depend upon supernatural forces. The ultimate solution to our problems and the ultimate liberation from suffering lies exclusively in the ordinary.

Magic Is an Expedient Means for Teaching

The general public usually accepts magic more readily than reason. Under unusual circumstances, highly esteemed Buddhist masters throughout history utilized magic as an expedient means of spreading the Buddhist teachings. During the East

Han Dynasty, under the regime of Emperor Ming, Buddhism was introduced into China. Daoists resisted and challenged the Buddhist missionaries to a public duel of magic. The Emperor presided over this historic contest. He ordered two rows of tables to be placed in a great hall. The Buddhist scriptures and some of the Buddha's relics were placed on one row of the tables and the Daoist scriptures on the other. The Daoist priests entered dramatically, either by flying or by materializing magically. The Buddhist representatives Kasyapamatanga and Dharmaraksa slowly walked into the hall. The crowd had bet that the monks could not win against the Daoist priests. After both sides settled into their respective seats, the Daoist priests initiated the contest by using spells in an attempt to incinerate the Buddhist scriptures, but nothing happened. Instead, the Buddha's relic emanated a brilliant light. When the light reached the Daoist scriptures, the books instantly caught on fire and were quickly destroyed. At this point Kasyapamatanga flew up into the sky and spoke:

> A fox cannot be compared to the majestic lion;
> A lamp cannot match the brilliance of the sun and the moon;
> A pond cannot be as all-encompassing as the ocean.
> A hill cannot be as tall and grand as a mountain.
> The clouds of the Dharma cover the world,
> Enabling those with seeds of goodness to sprout and grow.
> The manifestation of unusual magic powers
> Is but a means for delivering the ignorant throughout [the world].
> —*The History of the Buddhist Patriarchs* [Fozu Lidai Tongzai]

He continued, "This verse means that the spirit of Buddhism is as dignified and majestic as the lion, the king of all animals. How can the fox-like, crooked Daoist tendencies compare?

Daoism is like an oil lamp; its wisdom cannot match that of Buddhism, brilliant as the light of the sun and the moon. A pond cannot hold the vast quantity of water in a great ocean; a small hill is no match for a great and tall mountain; how can Daoism compare with the transcendent realm of Buddhism? The auspicious clouds of the compassionate Buddhist teachings cover the world, enabling those with roots of goodness to sprout and grow the seeds of bodhi, eventually attaining the supreme fruit of the Buddhahood. Today I have used magic as an expedient means to convert ignorant living beings to the right path, so that they may attain the supreme fruit of the Buddhahood. Magic, however, is not the ultimate way."

Upon hearing Kasyapamatanga's words and witnessing the extraordinary power of the monks' magic, the Daoist priests were petrified. They tried to escape, but their magic powers failed completely. Emperor Ming was impressed by the virtues and powers of Kasyapamatanga and Dharmaraksa. He then built four temples within the city and three temples outside its boundaries for Buddhist nuns and monks. This was the beginning of pure cultivation and freedom to practice for monks and nuns in China. Because of this magic duel, Buddhism finally planted its seed in China, where it eventually took root and blossomed. Again, although the use of magic is not the final solution, when it is used with a foundation of virtue and the intent to benefit others, it can be an expedient means for spreading the teachings.

THE CULTIVATION AND USAGE OF SUPERNATURAL POWERS

Is the gift of magic beyond the reach of the general public? Where do we discover its presence and beauty? Magic is all around us. We should appreciate the true meaning and wondrous application of magic in each moment of our lives. Simple, ordinary life contains bountiful and delightful magic that we should learn to enjoy. For example, when we look at beautiful flowers, green grass, or the bright moon on a clear night, our spirits naturally soar, and we feel joyful. Is this not magic? When we wish to please another person, we can say a few words of praise, and this person will beam with delight. If we say harmful words, however, the other person may shrink in defeat and pain. Is this not the magic of language? Human emotions, such as happiness, rage, sadness, and joy, are they not all magic?

When we wish to watch a television program, we push a button on the remote control, and instantly the screen projects the image for us. This image may arrive from far away—even from a distant country via satellite transmission. Is this not celestial vision? When we pick up a telephone, we can hear voices from afar, even through vast and dense obstacles. Is modern communication not celestial hearing? Airplanes allow us to fly like birds, reaching any destination we desire. Do we not have the miraculous power to travel anywhere and overcome the constraints of distance? If we are alert and mindful, we will discover that our everyday existence is magic. It is when we are inattentive that magic is no longer apparent and wondrous.

Magic also exists in nature. For example, when dark clouds fill the sky, raindrops will begin to fall. Sometimes, even when the sun is shining, large raindrops still fall. Is this phenomenon not magical? Depending on the interaction of different pressure systems, gentle breezes, wind gusts, hurricanes, thunderstorms, hail, or even snow may occur. The seasons change and enable all living beings to continue their growth and maintain a harmonious ecological balance. All of these amazing changes in nature can be regarded as magic.

In our daily lives, magic is also the accumulation of experience, the expression of human wisdom, and the skillful utilization of resources. The terms printed on the Chinese calendar, such as "spring begins," "excited insects," "rain water," "autumnal equinox," "severe cold," etc., all describe seasonal periods as documented through the experience of countless generations. These detailed observations represent a precious inheritance from our ancestors. Farmers use their years of experience to predict weather and to decide the proper time for planting and harvesting. In our society, many experts have already warned us about the consequences of unchecked population growth, the destructiveness of environmental pollution, and the possibility of an energy shortage. This foresight into the coming years allows us to plan for the future now. How can all these people see into the future? Experience empowers them to predict the future. Experience is powerful magic.

A decision made through wisdom is also a form of magic. Zhuge Liang could predict the future accurately and devised unusual strategies to secure a stronghold for the Kingdom of Shu during the Period of the Three Kingdoms. The Ming philosopher Wang Yangming advocated "seeing things through one's conscience" and "using actions to accompany knowledge in predicting the future." History is full of wise individuals who see the changes of time and intelligently predict trends of the future. They are capable of making these predictions because of their wisdom. Magic is a beautiful expression of wisdom. When we face difficulty, if we analyze the situation and devise solutions using wisdom, the difficulties will not be as devastating and will be easily resolved. Is this not magical?

The accumulation of human knowledge that leads to many scientific advances is also a form of magic. The moon has been regarded as romantic, mysterious, beautiful, yet out of our reach. Now, with a meticulously designed spaceship, we have landed on the moon and have walked on its rugged surface. Anyone living before the twentieth century would certainly consider this an act of magic. With the abundant recent advances in medical technology, we now have many treatments that would be regarded as magic to our ancestors. If our skin is badly damaged, we may undergo a skin graft from another part of the body that allows us to heal. If our kidneys become unhealthy or our hearts fail to function, we may receive an organ transplant from an unknown donor. If we cannot see, we may even benefit from a cornea transplant. The success of test tube babies opens a new door for human reproduction. All these advances would be considered a type of startling magic to our ancestors. We have invented cloud seeding to manipulate the weather and airplanes to swiftly transport us. Are we not calling forth the rains and flying freely in space now? Magic is not unique to the spirits and celestial beings. If we use our knowledge wisely, we can create endless miracles in our worldly lives.

Since magic is so closely connected to us, how can we attain magical powers? In Buddhism, acquiring magic is not considered difficult. The important question is, upon what should magic be based? There are four foundations upon which magical power must rest: 1) compassion, 2) the precepts, 3) patience, and 4) the ordinary.

Compassion

According to the *Mahaprajnaparamita Sastra*, "bodhisattvas abandon the five desires and attain the different states of meditation. Out of compassion for all beings, they acquire magical powers and use them to benefit all beings. They perform miracles to purify people's minds. Why? If one does not perform the extraordinary, many people cannot be impressed and saved." Unlike sravakas and pratyeka-buddhas, who are liberated from rebirth and choose to remain removed from humanity, bodhisattvas, though they have eradicated all defilements, choose not to enter into nirvana for their love of all beings. Bodhisattvas pledge the great bodhi vows and acquire magic so that more living beings can be saved.

Why is magic needed for emancipating people? Employing these powers is sometimes necessary because most people are ignorant. They do not cherish the truth of the ordinary, nor can they see the path to enlightenment in the commonplace. They are deeply influenced only by the extraordinary. Bodhisattvas have to use miracles as an expedient means to impress people and open their hearts and minds. Thus magic serves as a tool for bodhisattvas, but Buddhahood is the true goal of the bodhisattva journey. After all, to cultivate oneself without compassion is to follow a grievous path. Attaining magical power without compassion is like adding a new weapon to a ferocious creature's arsenal. The resulting harm will be even greater. Examples of the cultivation of magic without compassion include the Buddha's cousin Devadatta using magic to damage Buddhism, and evil spirits using magic to harm innocent people. Therefore, before one starts to learn magic, one must observe the prerequisite of nurturing one's compassion. Without compassion, one should not learn magic, for it will only be abused.

The Precepts

Magic based on the pure precepts means that practitioners must uphold these instructions for wholesome and right living. Following the precepts is one aspect of the threefold training of Buddhists. The body and mind should rest on the precepts, focusing on their perfect ability to lead us down a virtuous path. By accepting the precepts, we can distinguish right from wrong, and determine what should be done and what should be avoided. When we faithfully maintain the spirit of upholding the precepts, we will guard our actions and will not use magic to harm others. We will only use magic as an expedient means to help accomplish beneficial deeds aligned with the precepts. Therefore, when we learn magic, we must strictly honor the precepts. Otherwise, the resulting magic will become the destructive power of evil.

Patience

The mental discipline of patience is an important foundation for the use of magic. If the virtue of patience is not adequately developed in us, we can easily lose control. When we are empowered by magic in this agitated state, we may be prone to misuse magic in order to attack those we dislike or those who stand in our way. Used in this fashion, magic is nothing but another sharp weapon for suppressing others. We must learn to be patient and never use magic unless absolutely necessary. Even then, any show of magic is strictly a means of upholding righteous truth and benefiting more people than other means would permit.

The Ordinary

According to the sutras, "The ordinary is the Way." Buddhist teachings are intended for the purification of character and cultivation, not for encouraging the eccentric or unusual. When the mind rests in everyday commonness, its power can last for all of eternity. In contrast, magic is for the moment only. Magic cannot eliminate the hindrances that bind us to our fundamental defilements, nor can it lead us to ultimate liberation in life. Only through seeing the ultimate truth of the teachings in our everyday lives and purifying ourselves in the quest for total liberation can we experience true magic. Even the highly cultivated Buddhist sages and arhats who practice the power of eradicating all defilement cannot do so without first completely integrating their lives with the truth of Buddhist teachings.

My maternal grandmother became a vegetarian and started diligent cultivation in Buddhism around age seventeen. She took care of me from my early childhood. Her character influenced me greatly and helped nurture the cause for me to become a monk. I recall that as a young child I stayed with my grandmother the majority of the time. I was always awakened by the incredible wave-crashing sounds that resounded from her stomach at night. As a curious child, I asked, "Grandma, why does your stomach make such sounds?"

She replied confidently, "This is the result of cultivation."

After becoming a monk, I studied with many Buddhist masters. None of their stomachs ever made any sounds. Could these masters not be as spiritually cultivated as my grandmother? As I grew up, I eventually realized the answer. After seven or eight years, at age twenty, I returned home one summer to visit my grandmother. I saw her sitting alone under a tree. I sat next to her and asked, "Grandma! Can your stomach still make those sounds?"

"Of course. How can I lose the result of my cultivation?" Grandmother replied with confidence.

I asked her pointedly, "What is the use of a sound-making stomach? Can it eradicate defilement and sorrow, develop virtue and morality, and stop the rounds of rebirth?"

Grandmother was stunned and did not know how to reply. Just then an airplane with a roaring engine flew overhead. Relentlessly, I continued, "That airplane engine can make a much louder sound than your stomach. Tell me, how does a stomach making noise contribute to a person's life?"

After listening to my questions, Grandmother was startled and confused. Silently she stood up and went inside the house. Now decades have passed. Whenever I recall my grandmother's confused and disappointed expression, I feel deeply apologetic. Although her unusual skill could be considered magic, a temporary skill at best, it was nonetheless the fruit of decades of diligent cultivation. Her lifelong adherence to vegetarianism may have contributed to her unique ability. How could I have been so insensitive as to damage her confidence with my merciless interrogation? However, despite my awkward approach, I believe that she eventually appreciated my wholehearted intent to guide her in the correct way of practice concerning the ordinary.

THE BUDDHIST PERSPECTIVE ON SUPERNATURAL POWERS

Magic is hope in times of trouble; it is the savior during upheaval; it is an expedient means for teaching. Magic must be experienced in ordinary living. To conclude this chapter, we are going to further examine the Buddhist perspective on the limitations of magic and the supernatural. Thus far, I have explored many teachings and ideas about what magic *is*. In this final section, I will share four points that discuss what magic *is not*: 1) the ultimate, 2) a force that mitigates karma, 3) superior to virtues, and 4) a practice that surpasses emptiness.

Magic Is Not the Ultimate

According to the sutras, even though two thousand years have passed, several of the Buddha's disciples still live amongst us. Venerable Pindolabharadvaja is one of these followers. He is one of the sixteen disciples named in the *Amitabha Sutra*, and he has attained the holy fruit of arhat. Why would an arhat remain here and not enter nirvana? He is still here among us because he once showed off his magic in front of a group of faithful devotees. On this occasion, he was in a jubilant mood, and called to the practitioners, "Do you think flying in the sky is magical? I will show you something spectacular!"

He then jumped up into the sky and performed many miraculous feats. The faithful people were all impressed and praised him unceasingly. Upon learning about this incident, the Buddha was very displeased. He asked the venerable to come forth and admonished him, "My teachings use morality to change others and compassion to save living beings. They do not use magic to impress and confuse people. You have misused magic today. As punishment, I order you to stay in this world, to work for more merits, and to repent for this misbehavior before entering nirvana." Because the venerable misused magic, he must continue to live and suffer in this worldly realm.

Another example involves Chan Master Yin Feng, who was

mentioned earlier in this chapter. He was very humorous and full of Chan surprises. One day, while he was lecturing on the subject of life and death, he asked his disciples, "Have you seen people die during sitting meditation?"

His disciples replied, "Certainly. One Chan master passed away during sitting meditation."

Next, the Chan master asked, "Have you heard of people dying while standing?"

"Yes, we have. The family of Venerable Fu all died while working their farm," his disciples replied.

The Chan master then asked, "How about seeing anyone dying while standing on his head?"

With astonishment, his disciples replied, "That we have never seen or even heard of before."

The Chan master said, "Fine. In that case, I will show you." He then stood on his head and entered nirvana. His disciples were both shocked and saddened. They hurried to make funeral arrangements to honor their Chan master but encountered a difficult problem. When they attempted to move the master's body, they found it as immovable as a steel pillar. No matter how much force they applied, they could not lift it off the ground. Nobody knew what to do until the master's sister arrived. She was a highly cultivated nun and scolded the Chan master, "You used magic to confuse people when you were alive. Do you still want to use the same trickery to impress others at death? Come down now!"

Strangely, the body fell on command. Although this tale demonstrates a rather lighthearted misuse of magic, the Chan master's intent was not to impress others with his magic. Rather, he wanted others to see how Chan practitioners could treat the state of death with total control and freedom. Still, magic is not the ultimate method to relay such teachings.

Magic cannot increase our virtue or offer immediate enlightenment, and its careless use will only build more obstacles to emancipation. The practice of virtue is the only sure and steady approach toward the Buddha Path.

Magic Cannot Mitigate the Force of Karma

The strongest force in this world is not magic. Instead, the prevailing catalyst to all circumstances is the force of deeds, or *karma*. In Chinese history, there once was an uprising in which millions of people were slaughtered. There was a saying at the time of the massacre: "Rebel Huang will kill eight million. If you are in that number and it is your turn you will never escape." The legend held that this rebel actually did kill eight million people before he was finally suppressed. Regardless of whether this story is factual or mythical, let us ask what was meant by "that number" and "your turn." These phrases express the truth that no one can escape karma. The citizens who experienced that catastrophe during the uprising shared a common karma, which had to be repaid with blood. Magic cannot overcome the manifestation of karma. We must reap what we have sown. There is no escape.

Once, King Virudhaka of Kosala was attacking the Buddha's motherland, Kapilavastu. Maudgalyayana, foremost in magic among the Buddha's disciples, volunteered to save the Sakya clan. The Buddha replied sadly, "Maudgalyayana, this is the Sakya clan's karma and they have not repented for it. Today, they will have to bear the consequences for their deeds. Although they are my own family, even my magic cannot spare them."

Maudgalyayana did not believe the Buddha. He flew into the city, which was completely surrounded by troops. He picked five hundred Sakya clansmen and magically put them in his almsbowl. He flew out of the city and happily came before the Buddha. He said, "Lord Buddha. Look! I have saved a group of your clansmen."

However, upon peering into the bowl, he was shocked and

dismayed to see that the clansmen had turned into a pool of blood. Even Maudgalyayana himself, who was renowned for his magic, could not overcome or avert the force of karma. He could fly freely into the heavens and had even ventured into hell to save his mother. Yet, despite his magical abilities, a stone thrown by heretics eventually killed him. How can a venerable with such great magic be so easily killed by a stone? Many of the Buddha's disciples were perturbed and angry. The Buddha spoke to the disciples: "Magic cannot mitigate the force of karma. It is Maudgalyayana's karma to be killed by the stone thrown by heretics. You should not doubt the limit of magic. However, it is more important to diligently purify your actions, speech, and thought."

Magic is not all-powerful. One must not think that magic will eliminate all fear or erase all troubles. The force of prior karma cannot be influenced by magic. If we rely only on magic, we will worsen our situation and may even lose our lives.

Magic Is Inferior to Virtue

Beginning students in Buddhism are extremely attracted to magic. When they learn about someone who has had a supernatural experience, they flock to see this person. They usually overlook the cultivation of virtue in daily living and the presence of magic in ordinary living. Wisdom only comes from deep mental concentration developed through meditation, and successful meditation relies on upholding the precepts in daily life. If we are serious students of Buddhism, we must start from the foundation of morality, not magic.

Do you really think magic will automatically make your life happier? As long as we cannot read minds, even though people may hate us and curse us, we remain oblivious to it and suffer no insult or pain. If we could read minds, then we would know when someone is totally immoral, that another person is hateful, and that still another is full of devious ideas. We would feel uncomfortable and overwhelmed with grief among these people. Even when we wished to be spared from such negative thought patterns, we would still receive the information. Each and every day would be long and somber. Suppose that we were about to die tomorrow but remained unaware of this impending change. Today would still be a joyful and carefree day. If we had the power of knowing the future and learned that death awaited us in twenty years, from this day on we would anxiously live our lives under the shadow of death. If we had celestial vision and discovered that our loved one was having an affair, we would be consumed by jealousy, and life would be miserable. If we did not know about this tragedy, we might instead continue to live with happiness and contentment. If we had celestial hearing, we might find our most trusted friends reviling us behind our backs, and we would certainly become enraged by this betrayal. Without celestial hearing, we may enjoy continued peace and confidence.

Clearly, magic would not necessarily make life better. Morality and virtue are the true, inexhaustible treasures. We should not have access to magical powers before we are accomplished in high virtue and morality, for we may not be prepared for its revelations. A life of virtue is superior to a life of magic.

Magic Cannot Surpass Emptiness

Magic is in the realm of phenomena. The prajna-wisdom of Buddhism is in the realm of emptiness, which is everywhere and not bound by anything. When there is experience in life, experience is magic. When there is wisdom in life, wisdom is magic. When we have different capabilities in life, those capabilities are magic. The truth of emptiness permeates life; the truth of emptiness is also magic. The wisdom of emptiness is very profound. It is not void or annihilation as most people commonly believe. Emptiness allows existence. It is the source of all phenomena. For example, the empty space in various Buddhist temples around the world can accommodate practitioners in their worship, as well as ceremonies and services. When our hearts are as broad as the universe, we too have the capacity for everything. Emptiness is the most powerful force. Magic cannot compare with its boundlessness and inexhaustibility.

Once, Chan Master Venerable Dao Shu settled next to a Daoist temple. The Daoist priests were very irate at his presence and used every kind of magic and trickery to scare him away. Almost all of the residents were frightened and sought refuge elsewhere. However, the Chan master remained unmoved. After twenty years, the Daoist priests gave up. People asked, "What magic did you use to outlast those Daoist priests?"

The Chan master replied, "Oh, nothing. I used emptiness to beat them. Daoist priests have magic and tricks. 'Having' is finite; it is exhaustible, bound, and measurable. I do not have any magic. 'Not having' is infinite, inexhaustible, boundless, and immeasurable. Therefore, emptiness (not having) can overcome magic (having) by being broader, greater, higher, and superior."

In Buddhism, emptiness is the basis for all existence. It is much more powerful than magic. The wisdom of emptiness is more profound than magic. We are better off attaining the truth of emptiness, rather than the power of magic. Understanding the truth of emptiness is far more essential and valuable than being preoccupied and dazzled by magic. After all, to see emptiness as the ultimate cause and condition for all existence is to realize one of the core perspectives in Buddhism—the Law of Cause and Condition. The following chapter will examine this very important Buddhist truth.

CHAPTER FIVE

CAUSE AND CONDITION

THE LAW OF CAUSE AND CONDITION

More than 2,500 years ago, Sakyamuni Buddha "was born into this world to create the causes and conditions of a major mission." This mission, or body of causes and conditions, is what we now commonly refer to as "Buddhist Dharma," the Truth realized by the Buddha. In this chapter, I will first introduce the Buddhist perspective of causes and conditions and then discuss four central components, which include: 1) causes and conditions in human relationships, 2) identifying the existence of causes and conditions, 3) the different levels of causes and conditions, and 4) how to multiply and improve wholesome causes and conditions.

Buddhist teachings differ from scholastic inquiry or academic philosophies based on empirical knowledge. Typically, scholastic inquiry focuses on the explanation of appearances; it is an interpretation based on the name and form of phenomena. In contrast, Buddhism emphasizes the penetrative understanding of the *nature* of phenomena; it is ultimate and complete.

For example, let us examine my hand. Common knowledge holds that it is a hand. Medical science looks at it as a structure of bones, muscles, nerves, and cells. Literature defines the hand in terms of style, gesture, and expression. A philosophical interpretation of the hand regards it as the embodiment of destiny and a symbol of friendship. In physics, the extension and contraction of the hand is force and movement. From these perspectives, the hand is regarded as real, as something that truly exists.

In contrast, the Buddhist view of my hand is like a penetrating x-ray which reveals that the hand is really only an illusive form, unstable in nature and subject to eventual decay and disappearance. It is a phenomenon that is ultimately empty in its nature. Suppose I extend my hand and make a grasping motion. Common knowledge and intellect would say that I have grasped some air and dust particles in this gesture. From the Buddhist point of view, the grasp—and on a larger scale, life—is "like a dream, illusion, or shadow, like the dew or lightning." It is a phenomenon that only exists because of the combination of certain causes and conditions.

Considering these different viewpoints, we can see that human perspectives are often narrow and confined. They can hinder us from looking at the world in the radiance of ultimate wisdom that does not attach static labels or definitions to phenomena. Worldly happiness and suffering do not have an absolute existence of their own. Both arise only because of the differentiation we make in our perceptions and the judgments we apply to cognition. In order to truly understand and accept the Buddhist teachings, we need to change our perspectives. We must move beyond superficial phenomena and into the ultimate reality of "suchness," illuminate our prajna-wisdom, and sow bodhi seeds. Only then will the Dharma water of samadhi flow into the spiritual fields of our hearts.

A Buddhist sutra tells a story that exemplifies the nature of perception and judgment. There once was an old woman who cried without ceasing. Her elder daughter was married to an umbrella merchant, while the younger daughter was the wife of a noodle vendor. On sunny days, she worried, "Oh no! The weather is so nice and sunny. No one will buy any umbrellas. What will happen if the shop has to be closed?" These worries troubled her greatly. She could not help but cry for the older daughter's misfortune. When it rained, she would cry for the younger daughter. She thought, "Oh no! The weather is so ugly and dreary. You cannot dry noodles without the sun. Now there will be no noodles to sell. How will they survive?" As a result, the old lady lived in perpetual sorrow. In sun and in rain, she always grieved for one of her daughters. Her neighbors could not console her and jokingly called her "the crying lady."

One day, the old woman met a monk. He was very curious as to why she was always crying. She explained the problem to him. The monk smiled kindly and said, "Madam! You need not worry. I will show you a way to happiness, and you will grieve no more."

When the crying woman asked the monk to share his idea, the master replied, "It is very simple. You simply need to change your perspective. On sunny days, do not think of your eldest daughter not being able to sell umbrellas. Rather, think of your younger daughter, who will be able to dry her noodles. On those days, she will be able to make plenty of noodles, and her business will be very profitable. When it rains, think about your eldest daughter's umbrella store. She will sell many umbrellas, and her store will prosper."

The old lady understood the meaning of the monk's words, so she followed his instructions. After a while, she did not cry anymore; instead, she smiled every day, considering the good fortune of one or the other of her daughters. From the day she shifted her viewpoint, she became known as "the smiling lady."

Whenever we have worries and problems, if we can emulate "the crying lady" and change our perspective a little, we can transform worries and problems into happiness and fortune.

This does not require magical power. If we can comprehend a minute amount of the wondrous Dharma of Buddhism and apply it effectively during pivotal junctures in our lives, we can make breakthroughs in our understanding. We will then turn foolishness into wisdom and ignorance into enlightenment.

With even a small morsel of knowledge about Buddhism, most people know that Sakyamuni Buddha achieved enlightenment while gazing at the evening stars under a Bodhi tree on a "diamond" throne. When a bright shooting star streaked across the sky, what did the Buddha come to realize? He understood the ultimate reality of the universe and life. What then is the Truth realized by the Buddha? It is the *Law of Cause and Condition*, the *Law of Dependent Origination*.

If we can understand the Law of Cause and Condition and the Law of Dependent Origination, and if we can live by these two aspects of truth, we will enter the highest realm of the Buddha. We can then abandon all the pains and anxieties that are associated with this imperfect worldly existence that we create out of our unclear minds. The scripture teaches, "All phenomena arise out of causes and conditions; all phenomena cease due to causes and conditions."

What do we mean by causes and conditions? Causes and conditions are nothing other than human interactions and relationships. Relationships can be loving and respectful, antagonistic and competitive, good or bad. If we can grasp the Law of Cause and Condition, we can understand the rise and fall of sentient beings' welfare, the origin and extinction of existence, and the reality of the universe and humanity.

There are usually four ways people look at the eternal arising and ceasing of causes and conditions. These are each discussed in turn below.

Without Cause, Without Condition
Commonly held beliefs about life include random chance,

divine design, and predetermination. These perspectives do not consider life from the standpoint of causes and conditions. For example, rocks do not normally produce oil, but suppose that someone accidentally mines fossil oil from rocks. Instead of analyzing the fossil oil and finding the causes of its formation, the person just assumes it is a random occurrence. Or, when a child overeats and chokes to death, instead of realizing that overeating has many logical and potential consequences that can be prevented, the family members lament the occurrence as destiny. Or perhaps an unsuccessful robbery attempt results in murder; the family of the victim simply blames it on predetermination.

The most misguided people are those who lay all responsibilities, and therefore the consequences, at the doorsteps of their god or gods. They deny the value of choice, the meaning of effort, and the importance of self-determination. This total reliance on destiny or predetermination negates the significance of self-help. These are erroneous and one-sided views that are not in accordance with the Law of Cause and Condition.

Without Causes, but With Conditions

Many people do not believe in past causes, conditions, and effects. They believe that life depends only on present conditions and current opportunities. They look at mishaps as the lack of proper conditions or as predicaments in which "Everything is in place except for the east wind."[1] Some siblings in a family may persevere and become successful. Others may simply give up and fail. They may blame their failure on the lack of opportunities or ill fate, overlooking their differences in education and character as well as and the influence of their own past experiences. Students in the same class may fin-

---

1. This saying refers to the famously wise minister and military strategist Kongming, who would have won an important battle except that a critical condition for winning was missing: the east wind.

ish with different grades and attribute the differences only to the present and apparent conditions of how much they apply themselves, overlooking the underlying causes of the variations in aptitude, intellect, and experience. This is only a partial and biased understanding of causes and conditions.

With Causes, but Without Conditions

In contrast, many people attribute their circumstances to causes, but not to conditions. For example, many talented people fail to live up to their potential due to the lack of proper conditions in which to exert themselves. When first entering the work force, they apply for jobs that call for experienced workers. When they are mature, they encounter openings that want only new graduates. Such situations happen all the time, but without proper understanding of the dynamic interplay of causes and conditions, one may be caught in a pattern of suffering or failure.

With Causes and Conditions

As shown in all the examples above, some people view causes and conditions as separate and independent. Sometimes they believe in causes but not in conditions, and at other times, they only accept the existence of conditions. These people fail to realize that causes and conditions are not static, but are instead forever changing in the space-time continuum, never standing still to wait for anyone. There is an old saying that illustrates this point:

> Good begets blessings; and evil will be punished. It is not that there are no consequences to our actions; it is just a matter of time before they are realized.

Consequences and new conditions are always produced by our acts, but the results are not always immediately evidenced. Consider, however, that although the force created by our evil acts is always present, the negative karmic ramifications in our lives can be diluted and softened through the careful construction of new, wholesome causes and conditions.

The views described above are biased and do not reflect the correct interpretation of the Buddhist view on causes and conditions. In Buddhism, we believe that causes, conditions, rewards, and punishments are all intertwined, one giving rise to the other and unable to exist with complete independence. All circumstances happen and all situations change because of the existence of causes and conditions.

In Buddhism, the common and most fundamental thread for all Dharma is the Law of Cause and Condition, regardless of whether it is practiced by followers of the school of Mahayana or Theravada, whether it is viewed from the perspective of principles or phenomena, or whether the perspective is worldly or transcendental. All phenomena in existence are the product of the proper mix of causes and conditions. The Surangama Sutra says, "All holy teachings, from elementary to profound, cannot depart from the Law of Cause and Condition." It is like building a house. We need bricks, wood, cement, and other materials. The construction can only be completed when one has all of the essential materials, the proper knowledge and skills, and all other prerequisites are met. It is illogical and against the basic principals of Buddhism to maintain that, without the essential conditions, a functional house can still be erected.

The following story shows how one man's ignorance of causes and conditions resulted in disaster when he attempted to have a successful party and managed to insult everyone he knew instead.

A rich man decided to throw a party. When only half of the guests had arrived, the chef asked if he could start to serve. The man told him to wait a little bit longer. After waiting a few hours, many important guests still had not arrived. Impatient and irritated, he insulted his guests by complaining, "Oh! It is not easy to throw a party. Those who should have come have not; those who should not have come are all here."

His seated guests were shocked. They thought, "Well, I guess I am not really invited. If I am not welcome, I may as well go home." Many of the guests quietly slipped away. Seeing that the party was dying, the rich man made another rude comment, "Oh! It is not easy to throw a party. Those who should leave have not. Those who should not have left are all gone."

Deeply offended by these disparaging words, every guest immediately stood up and left the party in a huff.

If we destroy our causes and conditions, and if we cannot seize and honor the moment presented to us by our own causes and conditions, success will be difficult to achieve. But with the appropriate causes and conditions, our endeavors will become successful. In the next four sections, I discuss and explain four points that can help us build good causes and conditions according to the Buddhist view on this core principle.

Cause and Condition and Human Relationships

Nowadays, it is popular to talk about "interpersonal relationships." With good interpersonal relationships, life seems to go smoothly. With animosity and constant confrontations, obstacles and problems abound. Events are the products of a combination of forces with "the major force called the cause; the lesser forces called conditions." Interpersonal relationships are forms of causes and conditions.

Even in a business situation, one must have harmonious human relationships. If we want to have a successful business, we must acquire sufficient capital, research the market, develop connections with people, and then establish investments. If we do our homework, our business will thrive; otherwise, it will surely face obstacles and be more likely to fail. These aspects of planning and action are the causes and conditions of a healthy business.

We must learn to be humble and appreciative of the relationships we have with others. Arrogance incapacitates even the most beneficial causes and conditions. One such example is the meeting between Bodhidharma and Emperor Wu.

Venerable Bodhidharma, the Chan school's first patriarch, traveled by sea from India to Canton, China during the Datong era of Emperor Wu (during the Liang Dynasty). The Emperor quickly sent envoys to accompany Bodhidharma to the capital. Emperor Wu, who wished to show off his past accomplishments, proudly asked Bodhidharma, "I have built numerous temples, published many sutras, and supported the sangha. How much merit do you think I have accumulated?"

Dampening the Emperor's arrogant enthusiasm, Bodhidharma solemnly replied, "None at all."

The Emperor was very upset. He continued to interrogate him, "What do you mean? I have performed so many good and outstanding acts of benevolence."

Bodhidharma replied, "Your Majesty! They are imperfect causes because you have tainted them with your conceit and hunger for recognition. They will only bring you minor rewards in the human and celestial realms. They are as illusive as shadows. They are only empty phenomena."

"Well! What then are real merits?"

"Do not become attached to the name and form of merits," Bodhidharma said with a smile. "Sanctify your thoughts. Realize the ultimate nature of emptiness. Abstain from greed and do not pursue worldly rewards."

The Emperor could not see the profound meaning behind these words. To show off his wisdom as the emperor of his people, he asked in his usual arrogant tone, "Between heaven and earth, who is the holiest?"

Bodhidharma saw through the vanity of the Emperor, and, not missing the opportunity to teach, replied, "Between heaven and earth, there are neither the holy nor the ordinary."

Emperor Wu asked incredulously, "Do you know who I am?"

Bodhidharma smiled softly, shook his head and said, "I do not know."

The Emperor had always considered himself a great benefactor of Buddhism. However, he was conceited and not truly sincere about learning the Truth. How could he possibly take such a slight from Bodhidharma? He reacted by flaunting his powers as the emperor and rudely sent Bodhidharma away. In so doing, he lost the causes and conditions to learn Chan from Bodhidharma and wasted an excellent opportunity for the advancement of Chinese Buddhism. Although he eventually regretted his behavior and tried to send for Bodhidharma, the conditions had been altered, and his wish remained unfulfilled.

Because the Emperor was egotistical and hungry for fame, he became caught up in the quest for merits and diverted from the Middle Path. He could not realize the ultimate truth that is "beyond true or false, beyond good or bad, and beyond holy or ordinary." Since the causes were improper and conditions were poor, it was no wonder that the encounter did not fulfill the Emperor's impure expectations.

It is written in the *Avatamsaka Sutra*, "All the water in the oceans can be consumed, all momentary thoughts as innumerable as dust particles can be counted, all space can be measured, and all the winds can be stopped. Despite these truths, the realm of the Buddha can never be fully described." To provide further clarity, I will describe an episode involving the Sixth Patriarch, Hui Neng, that also illustrates the Law of Cause and Condition.

When Hui Neng was young, he traveled thirty days from Canton to Hubei to learn the Dharma from the Fifth Patriarch. When they first met, the Fifth Patriarch immediately knew that Hui Neng had great potential and that the right causes and conditions were ripening. He asked, "Where are you from? And what are you seeking?"

"I have come from very far away, from Ling Nan. My only goal is to be a Patriarch and to become a Buddha," Hui Neng responded.

Hearing such a reply, the Fifth Patriarch was impressed. He wanted to test if Hui Neng had cultivated the right conditions and asked him pointedly, "You are only a barbarian from the south. How dare you wish to become a Buddha?"

Hui Neng replied calmly and confidently, "People may be from the south or north, but Buddha Nature is non-regional. When the right causes and conditions exist, anyone can become a Buddha. Why not me?"

Hui Neng's wisdom struck a chord with the Fifth Patriarch. He reflected for a moment, and then replied, "Okay! You are allowed to stay here and work. Report to the threshing mill."

Every day for the next eight months, Hui Neng used a huge axe to chop firewood. Every day, he wore stone weights around his waist to act as ballasts while he threshed the grain. Not once did the Fifth Patriarch visit him; never did he teach Hui Neng a single word. Hui Neng did not complain or become upset. It was late one night after these countless hours of toil when the Fifth Patriarch finally handed Hui Neng his robe and bowl, making him the Sixth Patriarch. The Fifth Patriarch explained the timing and reason for his decision with this verse:

> Those with sentience come to sow
> In fields of causation, fruits will grow.
> Ultimately, without sentience, there is nothing to sow.
> Without nature, there is nothing to grow.

What the Fifth Patriarch was expressing to Hui Neng through this verse is this: "When you first arrived from the distant land of Ling Nan to learn the Truth from me, the causes were ripe and you were sincere. The environment and conditions, however, were inadequate. Many people labeled you as barbaric, uncultured, and unfit for this reputable position. Because of your crude ancestry, many thought that they were more capable and worthy to receive the robe and crown. I first had you polish and cultivate yourself for a period of time. Only now, with the proper conditions in place, will the populace acknowledge and respect your wisdom and ability. Only when the right causes and conditions were nurtured would I then transmit the teachings and honor you as the Sixth Patriarch."

From this story, we can see how causes and conditions greatly influence how people interact with one another. Without the appropriate causes and conditions, human relationships will be imperfect, poorly timed, and regretful. Events and relationships must await the wondrous maturity of causes and conditions. It is like planting flowers. Some seeds planted in spring may blossom in autumn. Others may take a year to bloom. Some varieties may take even a few years to flower and bear fruit. Each unique variety requires the right causes and conditions for its beauty to unfold.

To bring even greater clarity to the power of ripe causes and conditions, I will share a few more illustrations. Han Yu, a famous Chinese scholar of the Tang Dynasty, was demoted and transferred to the remote area of Chaozhou. Because this area was far removed and culturally unsophisticated, there were few learned scholars with whom he could converse. When he heard that the Chan Master Dadian was teaching in the area, he immediately went over for a visit. When Han Yu arrived, the Chan master was meditating, so he decided to wait outside. After a long wait, the master was still in meditation, and Han Yu became restless. He stood up and prepared to leave. The master's attendant suddenly said, "First, influence through meditative concentration, then eradicate arrogance with wisdom." For Han Yu, these words resonated like spring thunder, and he awakened to greater awareness and wisdom. Because timing and opportunity formed the right conditions at that moment, Han Yu was able and ready to recognize the teaching and learn the way of emancipation from the attendant.

In another example, several years ago, a female university graduate left Taiwan with high hopes and traveled halfway across the world to study for her doctoral degree in the United States. After a period of two years in the U.S., she found her life had very little meaning or direction, so she packed her bags and returned to Taiwan. From Taipei, she took a two-hour train ride to Hsinchu and became a Buddhist nun. This news story received a lot of attention when reported by the media. The famous Professor Liang Shih-chiu sighed, "If what she wanted originally was to renounce secular life and become a nun, all she had to do was take a two-hour train ride from Taipei to Hsinchu. There was no need to fly to America and waste all those years. Why spend all that time struggling and then choose to renounce?"

The causes and conditions of all human affairs parallel the unfolding circumstances that resulted in this woman's sudden renunciation of worldly life to become a nun. Events may come and go, people may meet and depart, but however random or worthless an experience may appear, there is always meaning in every circumstance and moment. The following Chinese saying captures this point well: "Without a bone-chilling freeze, how could plum blossoms have such a sweet fragrance?" The causes and conditions operating in this woman's life needed time to ripen in order for her to enter the monastery; her clear choice could not arise independently or prematurely. Everything must first have the right causes and proper conditions before results are produced and other favorable conditions are generated.

There is another story that illustrates these points well, the story of Chan Master Shitou Xiqian and his master Qingyuan Xingsi. When they first met, Qingyuan asked Shitou if he was a student of the Sixth Patriarch. "What did you take with you," he asked, "when you first went to study with the Sixth Patriarch in Caoxi?"

"My nature was complete," Shitou smiled. "I was not lacking anything prior to studying with the Sixth Patriarch in Caoxi."

"If everything was perfect, why then did you bother to go study in Caoxi?"

Shitou Xiqian replied definitively, "If I had not gone, how would I have known that I was not lacking in anything? How could I have known my true and free nature?"

As was also true for the young woman, Shitou Xiqian needed the proper conditions to unfold in order to understand the truth of his being. This wisdom was simply not accessible without the proper sequence and manifestation of causes and conditions.

All causes and conditions already exist in perfect form within each of us; they are not separate from our true nature. We can realize this truth in our daily living; we must simply wake up to its omnipresence. The continual flow of pure refreshing water is a form of causes and conditions. The blossoming of beautiful flowers is another form of causes and conditions. Parents raising us are our causes and conditions in family relationships. Teachers educating us are our causes and conditions in the pursuit of knowledge. Farmers, workers, and merchants supplying our daily needs are the causes and conditions for survival in this society. Drivers transporting us are the causes and conditions of traveling. Theater performances and television programs are the causes and conditions of entertainment. It is with these wondrous combinations of causes and conditions that we can live happily and freely.

The following verse celebrates the causes and conditions of human relationships and is usually found in temples next to statues of Maitreya Bodhisattva:

Before our eyes are people connected to us through condi-
tions;
As we meet and befriend each other,
How can we not be filled with joy?
The world is full of difficult and unbearable problems;
As we end up reaping what we sow,
Why not open our minds and be magnanimous?

How Do We Know Causes and Conditions Exist?

How can we be certain that causes and conditions really exist? How can they be realized and harvested? Let us first examine an incident in which a machine in a factory suddenly stopped functioning. A technician opened up the machine and discovered that a small screw was broken. The small screw was the cause. When all causes and conditions are not fully satisfied, the machine will not function. When we build a house, if a supporting beam is missing, the roof will collapse. When any ingredient of causes or conditions is missing, it can have a great impact on the circumstances of our lives.

Buddhism teaches that our bodies are made up of the combination of the four great elements: earth, water, fire, and wind. These four elements are the causes. We fall ill when they are not harmonized. Why does a flower fail to blossom? Why is a harvest not abundant? It could be a lack of proper conditions, such as inadequate irrigation or fertilizer. Even a space shuttle can be delayed by a simple computer problem. With the slightest variation in the set of causes and conditions, the resulting circumstances will be totally different.

No matter what problems or difficulties we may face, we must first examine the situation closely for any missing causes and conditions, and then employ our wisdom to positively affect the situation. We should not simply blame the gods or other people; if we do, we are avoiding personal responsibility and creating further troubles for ourselves. There are many situations in which couples fall in love, only to find that their families oppose the marriage, each criticizing the other party as unsuitable, poor, etc. When the conditions of support, approval, and love are absent, the marriage will probably face great turbulence and encounter painful obstacles. Other couples fall in love at first sight and get married with lightning speed, with the support and approval of their families. Their compatibility is sometimes beyond comprehension. The man may reason that it is a case of "Beauty is in the eye of the beholder." The woman may attribute their union to the fact that "With the right conditions, people come to meet from thousands of miles away." This is what we call ripened conditions.

I will share another story that illustrates the existence of causes and conditions. Once, King Milinda asked Bhiksu Nagasena, "Are your eyes the real you?"

Bhiksu Nagasena replied, "No!"

King Milinda further inquired, "What about your ears?"

"No!"

"Is the nose you?"

"No!"

"Is the tongue you?"

"No!"

"Does that mean your body is the real you?"

"No, the existence of the body is only an illusory combination."

"Your mind must be the real you, then."

"It's not, either."

King Milinda was annoyed and pressed him again, "Well, if the eyes, ears, nose, tongue, body, and thoughts are not you, then tell me, where is your true self?"

Bhiksu Nagasena grinned and replied with a question, "Is the window the house?"

The King was taken by surprise and struggled for an answer, "No!"

"How about the door?"

"No!"

"Are the bricks and tiles the house?"

"No!"

"Then what about the furniture and pillars?"

"No, of course not."

Bhiksu Nagasena smiled and asked, "If the window, door, bricks, tiles, furniture, and pillars are not the house, then where is the real house?"

King Milinda finally understood that causes, conditions, and effects cannot be separated or comprehended through a biased and partial view. A house can only be built with the presence of many causes and the fulfillment of many conditions. Likewise, human existence also requires the satisfaction and maturation of many conditions. If we know the Law of Cause and Condition, believe in its existence, plant good causes everywhere, and constantly cultivate advantageous conditions, we will enjoy smooth paths full of happiness and success. To conclude this section, I leave you with this verse to ponder:

If one understands the Law of Cause and Condition,
One can find spring in the midst of autumn frost and winter snow.

THE DIFFERENT TYPES OF CAUSES AND CONDITIONS

How many types of causes and conditions are there? We can examine this from four different perspectives.

Having or Not Having

The Law of Cause and Condition is not a matter of knowledge. It cannot be learned by research or through debates. It must be realized through the heart and mind amidst our daily living. If we come to understand the Law of Cause and Condition from real practice and experience, then this is "having" the true understanding of causes and conditions. Under the law of cause and condition, our true nature is all the same. The universe is us and we are the universe. If we only superficially comprehend the Law of Cause and Condition through intellectual speculation or as a mere expression of words, then this is "not having" a true understanding of causes and conditions. Such a superficial understanding will only be as futile as searching for fish on trees.

Wholesome or Unwholesome

Causes and conditions can be beneficial or harmful. Wholesome causes and conditions are beneficial. Unwholesome causes and conditions are harmful. Let us suppose a person lives to be a hundred years old. If he or she does not understand the causes of arising and ceasing—the ultimate reason for existence—and instead only comprehends causes and conditions superficially or incorrectly, he or she will then be easily enslaved by the changing environment and his or her own aging body, trapped in harmful causes and conditions. This sad person will expend a lifetime without the chance for individual liberation or the ability to help others become liberated. On the other hand, if a person has a firm belief and correct understanding, then all resulting causes and conditions will be bright and virtuous.

Internal or External

Causes and conditions can be internal or external. External causes and conditions are commonly noticed environmental factors. Internal causes and conditions are related to intrinsic value. As in the case of farming, the external factors may be the same, such as sun, water, and soil, but the harvest from different seeds may be quite different. Seeds, in this instance, have causes and conditions of different merit. Similarly, children from the same parents possess different temperaments, and students of the same teacher may perform with different levels of success or failure. External causes and conditions such as parents and teachers may be the same, but the internal causes and conditions, such as talent and aptitude, can be distinct and dissimilar. Therefore, we say that causes and conditions may be external and internal, and the natural and balanced interplay of the two is crucial for generating happiness and eradicating suffering. Although external conditions may be satisfied, if internal causes are inadequate or impure, the resulting effects will be undesirable and even harmful.

Correct or Erroneous

Causes and conditions can also be correct or erroneous. When some people become ill, they understand that illness is caused by disorders of the body or mind. They are willing to undergo treatment and can most likely be cured. This willingness to accept their plight and initiate a reasonable healing process is cultivating the correct causes and conditions. In contrast, when others are sick, they are confused about the true cause of their malady. They may be superstitious and feel a sense of irrational guilt, attributing their sickness to divine punishment. They rely on magical charms or special spells, or they ingest ashes from incense in an attempt to overpower the illness. When employing these nonsensical rituals, their illness will only worsen. These "solutions" are the result of an erroneous understanding of causes and conditions. Life may be smooth or bumpy, and obstacles may be many or few, but many of life's difficulties are actually rooted in misconceptions about the Law of Cause and Condition. We must know how to apply correct understanding and eliminate erroneous views.

To further deepen one's understanding of the Law of Cause and Condition, which encompasses the dynamic interplay between causes, effects, and conditions, it is important to understand the four levels through which we may all progress as we seek and encounter ultimate truth. They are right understanding, cause and condition, sunyata, and prajna. These four stages, discussed below, outline the steady process of development that people can experience as they come to realize the Law of Cause and Condition in clearer and more expansive terms.

Right Understanding

As ordinary people, we can understand the Law of Cause and Condition at the level of right understanding. Most of us have experience and intellect that enable us to observe and affirm causes and conditions in the world. When confronted with sickness, distress, or misfortune, we are able to determine the causes and can therefore liberate ourselves from suffering. This is the understanding of causes and conditions from a worldly perspective.

Cause and Condition

Those who have reached the level of arhat have realized transcendental truth. Since they know that the five aggregates (form, feeling, perception, mental formation, and consciousness) are empty, and they can thus abandon the hindrances of knowledge, they are elevated to a higher spiritual level. These wise practitioners understand that there is no absolute, and that all beings and phenomena are interdependent. They have realized the true nature of causes and conditions on a higher spiritual plane.

Sunyata

Sunyata, or emptiness, is the realm of bodhisattvas. They have realized both worldly and transcendental truth and can thus function in this world in a transcendental way. They realize that "Forms and smells are all Dharma. Words and quietude are ultimately Chan." When one can view the Law of Cause and Condition from the point of view of sunyata, then life is full of possibilities and nothing is unreachable.

Prajna

Prajna, the ultimate wisdom, is the realm of the Buddhas. Prajna is the wisdom, when one has achieved enlightenment, of one's original nature. It is the realm of one who has realized that true nature and phenomena are one. In this realm, there is no differentiation between worldly truth and transcendental truth. There is no distinction between self and others. Causes and conditions arise and cease of their own accord, just like the freely floating clouds in the sky. Everything is naturally integrated, seamless and fulfilled.

These four levels of understanding can be explained from yet another perspective. In order to produce music, beginning musicians must first study the notes of a piece. To generate each sound, they must look at each note on the score, become knowledgeable in the use of the instrument, and practice. They continue to practice until they can perform the piece with the aid of a musical score. This is the first level of performance. Similarly, when we still need to look at the phenomena of the external world for our understanding, we are at the level of right understanding.

When the performers have etched the music into their hearts and minds, they have expanded their level of practice. They can close their eyes and the notes will naturally appear in the mind. However, although they appear to perform without the physical presence of music sheets, their minds are still bound by the existence of the score. They still perform by following the notes and cannot freely express themselves musically. This is the second level of performance. When the internal understanding is in agreement with the external world, this corresponds to the second level of understanding, that of cause and condition.

As the performers continue to perfect their practice, they soon enter the realm where the boundary between the external and the internal vanishes. They do not need to depend on music sheets, nor do they feel the existence of the score in their minds.

When they perform, they become one with the music, forgoing their sense of a separate identity. The resulting music flows seamlessly, smoothly, and wonderfully. Although the performers no longer hold on to the musical score physically or mentally, they still play something that they have previously learned rather than a spontaneous composition. This level of performance corresponds to the third level of understanding, that of sunyata.

Finally, when the performers truly know and integrate their musical talent and the concepts of composition, they are musicians in tune with nature. They are one with the music, and they create beautiful compositions with every turn of their thoughts. Everything is music. Likewise, when one reaches the level at which each thought is prajna, the ultimate wisdom, and even each hand gesture is a wondrous discourse, one is then in the realm where there are no distinctions between the inside and outside, remembering or not remembering. Prajna represents the highest level of realization of the Law of Cause and Condition.

People nowadays tend to remain closed to even the first level, right understanding. We often look at the world in a cluttered and distorted way. We regard fame and fortune, the cause of many afflictions, as the highest and most pleasurable of accomplishments. Out of our equal, undivided, and unbound true nature, we insist on making distinctions and divisions of superiority. When the causes and conditions call for our peaceful mutual caring, cooperation, and coexistence, we instead become distrustful and hostile to each other, thereby generating conflict and disputes among ourselves. What is the point of all these troubles? The only way to free ourselves is to understand the Law of Cause and Condition correctly. When we can realize prajna, concentration, and wisdom, when we are not bound by phenomenal existence, and when we are able to let go of the fixation of *us* versus *them*, then we will be in complete accordance with the Buddhas, venture into the unlimited realms of the Dharma, and be wonderfully free.

HOW TO MULTIPLY AND IMPROVE
WHOLESOME CONDITIONS

Many people would probably agree that the greatest progress of the twentieth century has occurred in the area of human communication. It is also written in the sutras that, "Before achieving the Buddha Way, we must first cultivate favorable conditions with others." To cultivate favorable conditions is to build harmonious relationships and to establish good communication with other people.

One of the greatest treasures of life is the "cultivation of favorable conditions." Building plenty of good conditions is essential for an individual's happiness and for the welfare of the public in general. How, then, can we establish a multitude of good conditions with others?

To cultivate favorable conditions with others, people in the past have put up lanterns by the side of the road to make travel more safe and convenient for all. They have built rest stops for the weary and provided free tea to the thirsty. They have built bridges to establish connections with people from other shores. They have dug wells to provide good living conditions for everyone. Others have offered a kind word or a gift to foster good conditions with another. If your heart is full of pure and kind intentions, good conditions will open up everywhere. Here are some suggestions for cultivating favorable conditions with others:

1) *Monetary Assistance*—We can donate money as a way to build good conditions with others. Not only does it show our concern, it may even save a life. A monetary gift does not need to be substantial to bring joy or convenience to others. For example, if there is a car accident on the road,

someone may need a coin to call for emergency assistance. If you offer a coin, the person can make the life-saving call. Paramedics and physicians will then arrive and provide assistance to the needy victims. Your coin will have built a multitude of good conditions with others.

2) *Kind Encouragement*—When others are frustrated, a word of encouragement can bring them immense hope. When others are disappointed, a word of praise can refresh their positive outlook on life. There is a saying that "A kind word is more valuable than the gift of royal attire; a harsh word is more severe than the fall of the ax." There are times that a few kind words can bring great joy and peace to everyone.

3) *Meritorious Deeds*—A small gesture or even a simple thought can have tremendous impact when offered with sincere care. In Holland, there once was a child who, walking home one evening, noticed a small hole in one of the dikes that keep the land from flooding. He saw the sea water slowly seeping in and knew that if the hole were not patched up immediately, the dam would break before dawn and the town would be flooded. Since he could not find anything to patch the hole, he stuck his finger into the hole to stop the leak. He patiently stood by the dike throughout the windy and rainy night. The entire night passed and not a single person walked by the dike. In the morning, he was found almost frozen stiff, with his finger still tightly stuck in the hole. The people were very grateful to him for the quick thinking and altruistic perseverance that had saved the lives and property of the entire town. Therefore, "Do not commit an act of atrocity just because it is minor. Do not pass up the opportunity to perform a virtuous deed just because it is small." A simple kind gesture or thought can save countless lives and build boundless virtue.

4) *Educating Others*—We can use our knowledge and training to cultivate favorable conditions with others. For example, each day, there are millions of teachers around the world who patiently teach and pass on their knowledge to the younger generations. They are instrumental in promoting national intellect and catalyzing growth. If you show someone a minor skill, it can become his or her means for future survival. If you impart to someone a word of wisdom, it can influence his or her entire life and serve as the guiding principle for how he or she interacts with others.

5) *A Helping Hand*—We can create favorable conditions and earn great respect if we accommodate others. The traffic officer helping an elderly person to cross the street becomes a model civil servant. The sales representative who kindly helps shoppers find what they need can make the customers' shopping experience a real pleasure. The young person who politely gives his seat on a bus to a disabled person gives us confidence in our society's future. From the way we assist others in our daily lives, without seeking glory or praise, we can gauge if we live in a truly progressive and developed society—one that will certainly thrive amidst the proper causes and conditions.

6) *A Warm Gesture*—Sometimes a smile, a nod, or a simple handshake can build unimaginable good conditions. Once, in Taiwan, an unemployed young man was wandering the streets near the Taipei train station, thinking he would commit suicide by running in front of a wealthy person's expensive car. Through this fatal plan, his impoverished mother would be able to collect some monetary compensation on which to live. Just as he was about to end his life, a beautiful and gracious lady walked by and smiled at him. He was so moved by her smile that he instantly dismissed the idea of

committing suicide. The next day, he found a respectable job to support his family, and no longer wanted to die. The simple yet profound smile managed to build great causes and conditions for the young man.

There are many stories of bodhisattvas, patriarchs, masters, and practitioners who have dedicated their lives to cultivating favorable conditions that have yielded wide-reaching benefits. In China, there are four famous mountains. Each mountain is a sacred site where a different bodhisattva inspires the teaching of the Dharma. These four bodhisattvas, to whom we commonly pay respect, are Avalokitesvara, Ksitigarbha, Manjusri, and Samantabhadra. Each of these four Bodhisattvas generates causes and conditions in a unique way.

Avalokitesvara Bodhisattva creates special conditions through kindness and compassion. This Bodhisattva brings universal salvation to all. Through Avalokitesvara Bodhisattva's kind heart and compassionate vows, all sentient beings may benefit from the Dharma and actualize the mind of compassion.

Ksitigarbha Bodhisattva supplies special conditions for all beings through his great vow. This Bodhisattva vows to deliver all sentient beings regardless of where they are: "Only when all beings are emancipated shall I attain enlightenment. As long as hell retains even a single being, I vow not to reach Buddhahood." For thousands of years, Ksitigarbha Bodhisattva's limitless vow has served as the guide for countless beings on the path of Buddhahood. It has also ignited an eternal light for the Buddhist teachings.

Manjusri Bodhisattva brings special conditions through his extraordinary eloquence to expound the ultimate teachings. He brings light to the blind and the Dharma to the ignorant. With great wisdom, the Bodhisattva has propelled Buddhism into the profound and wondrous realm of prajna. Buddhism in China has flourished through the wise teachings of Manjusri Bodhisattva.

Samantabhadra Bodhisattva makes special conditions through his diligent practice. The Bodhisattva shows us the Way with every movement of his hands and feet. With the raising of his eyebrows or the twinkle of his eyes, the Bodhisattva conveys profound teachings. In Chinese Buddhism, Samantabhadra Bodhisattva is an exemplary model and has established virtuous conditions for cultivating simplicity and striving for wholeness.

In addition to these four great Bodhisattvas, there are countless patriarchs, masters, and Buddhist practitioners who cultivate favorable conditions with others in their unique ways. The following paragraphs offer inspirational stories of eight people who devoted their practice and their lives to the benefit of all beings.

Through his unique style of calligraphy and his steadfast commitment to the precepts, Venerable Master Hong Yi cultivated favorable conditions with people. For those sincerely interested in Buddhism, he often used calligraphy as a means to inspire a lifelong affinity with Dharma wisdom. The Venerable master was diligent in his spiritual cultivation and strictly upheld the precepts. He never uttered a word to compromise the Dharma, nor committed an act in violation of the precepts. As expressed in the proverb "the luxuriant flowering branches in spring and the perfect full moon in the sky," he has set a highly regarded example in Buddhism.

With his meditative concentration, Venerable Master Xu Yun fostered wholesome conditions with others. He was immovable, in accordance with the ultimate reality of "suchness." His mind was clear, focused, and imperturbable. He propagated the Dharma without speaking at length about the teachings. Although he interacted with many people, he never uttered a superfluous word or engaged in idle chatter. His thoughtful and purposeful contributions in conversation, although scarce, were always of great benefit to the people he encountered.

Through teaching the Dharma, Venerable Master Tai Xu nurtured favorable conditions with people. He used a fluid combination of words to expound the great wisdom of prajna, making the Dharma easily accessible to people of many different backgrounds. He taught the sutras to awaken the confused and wrote helpful expositions to educate those seeking to enrich their spiritual practice. He traveled to all corners of China and helped to revive a declining Chinese Buddhism with the gift of his tireless teaching.

Master Shan Dao created favorable conditions with others through illumination and radiance. His spiritual practice was so developed and pure that brilliant light beamed from his mouth whenever he chanted. For the physically blind, he ensured that their minds saw clearly. For the mentally blind, he illuminated their minds with the dazzling light of wisdom. He brightened the dark and defiled human existence with his radiant light.

Through chanting, Venerable Master Yin Guang cultivated favorable conditions with others. He was continuously mindful and contemplative of the Amitabha Buddha, and he chanted the Amitabha Buddha's name incessantly. In this way, he guided the faithful to maintain a strong belief in the Western Pure Land and to form wondrous causes and conditions with the Amitabha Buddha.

Other examples include Elder Sudatta in India who selflessly gave alms to foster good conditions with people. He was well respected for building the Jetavana Monastery, which became the focal point of the Buddha's missionary work in Northern India. Chan Master Yongming Yenshou nurtured favorable conditions by compassionately setting captured animals free. He saved countless creatures from the pain of the slaughterhouse and the torture of fiery stoves. Master Long Ku used tea to cultivate favorable conditions with others. He helped to quench the thirst of exhausted travelers and gave them renewed energy to continue on their long journeys.

Society needs the unity of group efforts to thrive, just as the happiness of individual existence relies on the integration of the six senses. The fulfillment of our daily needs depends on the close cooperation of all professions working together to facilitate the relationship of supply and demand. In this way, we can live with joy, hope, and peace. We should be thankful for the blessings of causes and conditions and for all members of society who benefit others through kind and wholesome living. If we want to be successful and happy, we must always strive to cultivate favorable causes and conditions with all beings. We must do it for the present as well as for the future. We should also create favorable Dharma conditions with the Buddhas and bodhisattvas. We must treasure, build, and live within our causes and conditions. According to a Buddhist saying, "Coming from the ten directions, going to the ten directions, together accomplishing affairs in all ten directions; ten thousand people contributing, ten thousand people giving, together cultivating ten thousand favorable conditions." If we can do this, we will be able to attain Buddhahood and the wisdom of enlightenment.

CHAPTER SIX

LIFE AND DESTINY

Of all the issues we confront in life, we are generally most concerned with those related directly to us. In particular, many people focus a great deal of thought and attention on destiny. In many ways, the important perspectives we have examined in the previous chapters all culminate in Buddhism's rational treatment of this issue. Each of us thinks differently about destiny. When experiencing hardship, some people complain bitterly about their fate. Others believe in a predetermined and immovable destiny that governs all circumstances. A few are content with what they have; they are optimists and live carefree lives, accepting each moment as it unfolds. Ultimately, only a full understanding of such truths as emptiness, rebirth, and the Law of Cause and Condition allows us to truly appreciate the empowering approach towards life and destiny that Buddhism advocates. This is because, regardless of whether we find ourselves defeated by our circumstances or celebrating a blissful life, Buddhism teaches that we should not be passive and simply accept our destiny as something we cannot control. We should instead build and nurture positive causes and conditions so that our lives offer maximum benefit to ourselves and others. The Buddhist perspective on life and destiny includes four main questions, which are discussed below.

THE CAUSES AND CONDITIONS BEHIND DESTINY

From a Buddhist perspective, our destinies are not static or pre-determined. We directly influence destiny through the choices we make, and many events in our lives, whether grandiose or seemingly insignificant, can change our destinies. Some people's lives are changed because of a certain person. Others' lives may be altered because of a dollar. There are still others who took a different course in life because of a specific occurrence. Even a word or a thought can cause drastic changes in people's lives. Though trivial in itself, a fraction of a second can serve as a catalyst for tremendous impact. It is like a pebble thrown into the sea. A pebble is small, but the ripples it causes can permeate the entire surface. Similarly, a minuscule moment, whether it includes a person, a thought, or an event, can cause a person's destiny to evolve in a vastly different manner.

How a Person Can Change Another's Destiny

There are countless examples of how lives are changed by love for a certain person. Take the example of Wu Sanguei of the Ming Dynasty. When he learned that the rebel bandit Li Zicheng had kidnapped his beautiful mistress, Chen Yuanyuan, he was enraged and asked the tribe of Manchus for assistance. He opened the gates of the Great Wall of China and let the Manchus inside the country. Although he defeated the bandits and reclaimed his mistress, his destiny was totally changed, and he is considered a traitor in Chinese history. For the sake of one man's love for a woman, China once again came under foreign rule, and Chinese history was rewritten. Edward VIII, King of England, abdicated his throne for the love of Mrs. Simpson and became the Duke of Windsor. In "forsaking his country" for the love of a woman, his life was completely changed. Chou

Ling-fei, the grandson of the famous Chinese author Lu Xun, fled China so that he could marry Chang Chun-hua of Taiwan. In doing so, a new destiny unfolded in which many opportunities opened up and a bright future was established.

Destinies within the family unit can also be steered in new directions. Some parents sacrifice their entire lifetimes for the love of their children. In China, there is the legend of Wang Chun-er, who remained a widow her entire life in order to raise her son. When her son became a renowned government official, she was able to enjoy the fruits of her unwavering love and parental success. Conversely, many children give up their futures to care for their aged parents. In order to respect their parents' wishes, they forestall their own ambitions, live out the rest of their lives in passive servitude, and forsake an otherwise promising career.

Over the course of Chinese history, there were many loyal government officials and soldiers who were willing to repay the favors of their emperors and lords by giving up their lives. During the Warring States period, for example, a warrior named Yu Rang wished to repay his late lord Zhi Po for understanding him and providing him with opportunities. He swallowed charcoal to alter his voice, painted his body to disguise himself, and with this artificial identity assassinated Zhao Xiangzi, his late lord's enemy. Afterward, he turned his sword on himself and died. In history books, there are also cases of women who made tremendous sacrifices for the men they loved; yet their lives ended in tragedy because their lovers were corrupt and cruel. For example, there was a woman named Huo Xiaoyu who was fiercely in love with Li Yiqing and thought they would live happily ever after. However, the unscrupulous Li Yiqing unexpectedly abandoned her, devastating her and forever altering her destiny.

Is there someone who has made a significant impact on your life? Maybe someone you love? Someone you hate?

Destinies can change and history can be rewritten on account of a single person.

How a Dollar Can Change One's Destiny

A dollar can also change our destinies. The legendary Henry Ford left home at an early age to seek his fortune. With the one dollar his father gave him, he built an automobile empire. He started the world-famous Ford Motor Company and made a name for himself in history, as well as impacting society's ability to travel longer distances with greater convenience. A dollar not only changed one man's destiny, but that of the world.

There is a story that took place during World War II, in which a young soldier saved a woman from suicide by pulling her out of the water. Instead of thanking him, the woman cursed the young man. In response to his patient inquiry, the woman finally divulged her tragic life story. Her husband had been framed and unjustly sent to prison. She was left alone and penniless to tend to her husband's sick parents and their three young children. To buy medication for her sick mother-in-law, she pawned all her possessions for a silver dollar. But she was deceived by the pawn shop owner, who gave her a counterfeit coin. She believed that her only escape from her misery and helplessness was to die.

The young soldier felt very sympathetic and said to her, "What a tragic story. I have a silver dollar here; please take this to care for your family. Give me the fake silver coin so that others will not fall into the same plight."

Slipping the counterfeit coin into his pocket, the young soldier hurried on to report to duty. In a fierce battle, he was shot in the chest. Amazingly, the bullet hit the fake coin, leaving only a dent, and his life was spared. The young soldier clapped his hands and exclaimed, "Well worth it! This coin is worth a million."

With an act of compassion, a silver dollar rejuvenated hope and saved the woman and her family. It also protected the young soldier's life. The power of money, even as little as a dollar, is immense.

Without the right view, money can also affect people's destinies in treacherous ways. There is a saying, "A dollar can subdue a great warrior." Some people are willing to break the law for the sake of money, creating a great deal of trouble for themselves and others. Many young adults today do not understand the integrity and effort it takes to earn an honest dollar. They are envious of the glamour and success of others but are unwilling to maintain ethics and morality when striving for it. They just want a "fast buck" and may even resort to crime, including theft, burglary, fraud, and murder. Not only do they disrupt the safety and peace of society, they doom themselves to life in prison—or, worse yet, no life at all.

In contrast, there are also many righteous people throughout history who would rather maintain their moral standards than bow to the power of money. Among Chinese historic figures, Tao Yuanming stands out for his refusal to subordinate himself for five pecks (approximately thirteen pounds) of rice. Another exemplar, Qian Lu, although completely destitute, would not lower his moral standards to the level of corrupt officials.

Clearly, money can change people's lives. As each one of us has varying views about money, we use and invest money in different ways, resulting in drastically different circumstances and destinies. It is apparent that our choice to give or not give, accept or not accept money, depending on the circumstances, can dramatically affect our destinies for good or for bad.

How an Event Can Change One's Life

In addition to people and money, events can also affect human destiny. Thomas Edison invented the light bulb and became a world-famous, well-respected inventor. As he illuminated the world for all humankind, he freed us from the torment and inconvenience of darkness. With the option of perpetual light, just think how our destinies were changed! People's activities were suddenly no longer subject to the rise and fall of day and night. Alfred Nobel also affected human destiny by inventing dynamite. From one perspective, we can consider how much pain has been levied on the human race through the misuse of dynamite by dangerous power mongers. From another perspective, the Nobel Prize has been a catalyst for significant social progress and advancement in world civilization. How much good has it bestowed upon us? Many other events have also had the power to bring forth both great blessings and massive calamities.

Respected people in impressive and important positions sometimes face a destiny of demise because of their involvement in certain events. A former prime minister of Japan fell from the pinnacle of political power to criminal indictment after becoming involved in a bribery scandal. Although he had been the most powerful politician in Japan, he was not above the law and was sentenced to serve time in jail. In the United States, the Watergate scandal unseated the late former President Richard Nixon from the most coveted position in the world. An event can bring us extraordinary glories; it can also cause us deep embarrassment. We should exercise caution and build our destinies with ethical and moral actions.

In my own life, there is one experience in particular that I have never forgotten. It cemented my devotion to the cause of Buddhism. Regardless of the years that pass, each time I recall the incident I am moved and choked with emotion. I was brought up in a temple and had always lived a life of bare necessities. I had always been very healthy, but when I was about seventeen or eighteen years old, I became very sick. I was perpetually nauseated and vomited constantly. My life was in grave danger because I was unable to hold down any food for a month or two. I do not know how it happened, but somehow my master learned of my despair and sent over half a bowl of pickled vegetables. By today's living standards, there is nothing special about half a bowl of pickled vegetables. In those times of impoverishment, however, they were like a gourmet meal. I can still remember how I was filled with gratitude. My eyes welled up with tears as I finished the vegetables. After feeling the unspoken love and care of my master, I vowed to myself, "Master, to repay your kindness, I will dedicate myself to promoting Buddhism and spreading the Dharma so that all sentient beings can benefit." That half bowl of pickled vegetables gave me unending strength—my faith in Buddhism has been unmovable, and I have willingly dealt with whatever hardships that have come my way.

There are countless examples of past venerable masters who changed their destinies because of a single event in their lives. The Sixth Patriarch emerged out of his shell of ignorance while pounding rice. Chan Master Xiangyen Zhixian was enlightened while tilling the soil. Countless Chan masters understood the subtleties of Chan teaching upon seeing flowers blossom and then wilt. Countless Buddhists have achieved clear understanding at the sight of the rising sun and moon. Countless traveling monastics extinguished the flame of anger and hatred in their minds when looking at beautiful mountains and clear rivers. If we can reflect on the events around us carefully, we may see them from a completely different perspective. Then we may travel down very different paths, and our destinies will be changed and beautified.

How a Word Can Change One's Life

At times, we carelessly offer or receive words, assigning them very little value in shaping our lives. However, many wise people have experienced dramatic shifts in their destinies because they were open to the powerful changes that words can inspire. There are many wonderful examples in which "mere" words changed people's lives in incredible ways.

Before becoming a monk, Chan Master Danxia of the Tang Dynasty had planned to travel to the capital for the national examination. On the way there, he met a monk who advised him, "Taking the examination for government positions can only bring you worldly fame and fortune. You will be much better off going to study Chan instead. You may then attain emancipation from the mundane world." Hearing these words, Danxia changed his mind and went to the temple to study Chan and become a monk. Eventually, he became an eminent Chan master. The monk's words penetrated Danxia, waking him up from his worldly dreams and opening up an entirely new destiny for him.

Sariputra and Maudgalyayana, the Buddha's two famous disciples, give us another example. Before they became Buddhist monks, they were Brahman leaders. One day, while they were meditating, a disciple of the Buddha by the name of Asvajit passed them during his alms round. He was reciting to himself the verse the Buddha had taught him, "All phenomena arise out of causes and conditions; all phenomena cease due to causes and conditions. Lord Buddha, my great teacher, has always taught thus." When Sariputra and Maudgalyayana heard these words, they both felt as if they had just seen the first light of the morning emerging from total darkness. At that moment, they saw the world with profound inner knowledge and awareness. From overhearing a single verse, their wisdom sprouted, and they understood the truth of the universe.

Having just read the verse, "All phenomena arise out of causes and conditions; all phenomena cease due to causes and conditions," what do you feel? To us, it may seem ordinary. To the two wise men, however, it was an explosion. It was a key that shattered all confusion and opened up the truth of the universe. When they heard those words, they converted from Brahmanism to Buddhism. They became disciples of the Buddha and attained the fruit of arhatship. The power of words is immense.

Once someone asked the Chan Master Zhaozhou, "When the universe is annihilated, does the body still exist?" The Chan master nonchalantly replied, "Just let it go." After the encounter, the Chan master did not feel quite satisfied with his answer. He pondered, "When great calamities occur as the world undergoes the decaying process, will our bodies still exist?" Simply because he was not pleased with his reply, "Just let it go," the eighty-year-old Zhaozhou put on his shoes and journeyed many miles to seek the answer. Later, people would often refer to this episode affectionately as follows, "For a single sentence—'just let it go'—the monk traveled over thousands of mountains."

Are there not many people whose lives have changed because of a few words from their parents, friends, teachers, or loved ones? Sometimes a few words of encouragement can lift us up from the depths of depression. At other times, a few words of denouncement can sink us into the pit of pain. Kind speech is one of the Four Bodhisattva Persuasive Actions; we should speak kind words frequently. The use of kind words reflects well on us and is a form of generosity toward others. We should never underestimate the effect our words can have on transforming destiny; speak carefully and listen closely, and your life will yield great rewards.

How a Thought Can Change One's Life

Life can be changed by a person, a dollar, an event, or a word. A thought can also propel destiny in a brand new direction. It can enable one to become a sage or remain an ignorant fool. It can make a person reach all corners of the universe—from heaven to hell. Thus, it is extremely important to focus one's mind and to practice right mindfulness.

Cheng Feng-hsi, who was once named one of the ten most outstanding youths in Taiwan, was disabled from birth. Because he used his hands like feet, he was the subject of ridicule by his ignorant playmates. However, due to his conviction, "I will stand up," he was able to persevere in spite of his disability and go on to finish his college education. He is a model of someone who struggles hard to improve himself and maintains faith and loyalty to an inspiring thought. Helen Keller is another example. She grew up blind and deaf, encased in a world of silence and darkness. In order to repay her teacher's patience and mentoring, she worked incessantly to improve herself and thereby became a respected and courageous individual. Despite her disabilities, she was nevertheless able to tour the world giving presentations that raised the world's consciousness about the plight of the disabled. Royalty and world leaders were honored to see and hear her. With her endless efforts, Helen Keller brought hope and light to millions of blind and deaf people. Very easily, she could have been a victim of her obstacles, allowing them to control her and therefore ensure a bleak destiny. But with her steadfast notion, "I can do this," she brightened not only her own destiny but the destinies of many people. She became a symbol of hope for the unfortunate.

Throughout history, innumerable Buddhist masters have been able to endure severe hardships because of a single thought of devotion. They dedicated their lives to spreading the Dharma and allowed this devotion to guide all of their actions and lead them through difficulties. In the Tang Dynasty, there was the legendary Venerable Xuanzang. As a young monk, he realized that there was a shortage of translated Buddhist scriptures in China, which inspired him to make a pilgrimage to India in order to bring more Buddhist scriptures back to China. He lived in India for eighteen years, brought back numerous sutras, and became the renowned "Master of the Tripitaka." His idea changed his life, opening a new chapter in Chinese Buddhist history in which his contributions mark a milestone and his impact is timeless.

The Venerable Jianzheng of the Tang Dynasty was deeply impressed by the sincerity of student monks who came from Japan to China to learn about the Dharma, and consequently he thought of bringing Buddhism to Japan. During the course of twelve years and seven attempts, he grew old and blind, but even in his enfeebled state he would not abandon his idea. After countless hardships, he finally succeeded in reaching Japan to promulgate the Vinaya there. Even today, the Japanese methods of constructing houses are styled after the Chinese, and Japanese customs closely resemble Chinese customs. The use of chopsticks and certain agricultural methods, such as sowing and transplanting, were also introduced by the Chinese. Venerable Jianzheng was credited with bringing the Chinese way of life to Japan and was honored as the "Father of Japanese culture." The one thought of spreading Buddhism to Japan opened up a new path for him, helped to develop Japanese Buddhist culture, and altered the lifestyle of the entire country. The master's exemplary act of "never forgetting your initial determination to attain enlightenment" gives us a whole new dimension in understanding the potential for unlimited courage and perseverance. His unwavering devotion allows us to grasp more firmly the truth that a single thought can change the life of an individual, a community, and the world.

WHAT CONTROLS DESTINY

We lead different lives with diverse circumstances. Sometimes, when we witness another person's success, we find ourselves thinking of our misfortunes. We become discouraged and divert responsibility from ourselves, complaining, "It is all a matter of timing, luck, and destiny." When we are dispirited about our misfortunes, we place the blame on other people or gods and complain about divine arrangements. In reality, our destinies are not in others' hands. What then controls destiny? It is only ourselves. Yet, how do we actually control our own destinies?

Habits Control Destiny

There is a Buddhist saying, "Defilement is difficult to sever; the force of habit is even harder to change." Bad habits cause us endless misery in the present and the future. Poor habits can negatively influence our lives and destinies. Our reckless and mindless thoughts and actions develop into habitual forces and become obstacles to our enlightenment. A person with a hot temper often yells at others. If this becomes habitual, he will not have many friends that he can rely upon for comfort or help, so his chances of succeeding in life will be low. Some people are addicted to gambling and indulge in extravagance. They squander their family fortune, break up their families, and destroy their own lives and the lives of their loved ones. Others become addicted to lying or cheating and thereby betray others' trust. Although their selfish schemes may provide temporary gratification, they will eventually become isolated because no one will have faith in them.

Many of today's juvenile delinquents are from affluent families. They develop bad habits and actually consider stealing to be a hobby or an amusing game. Sometimes they even rob and kill others because the force of their habits grows stronger and consumes them. Not only do they hurt the welfare of others, they also ruin their futures. Bad habits are like narcotics; before long, they have perverted our souls, corrupted our lives, and destroyed our happiness. Considering these dire consequences, how can we not be careful?

Superstitions Control Destiny

Although we may think that superstition is a unique product of Eastern culture, it is also found in the West. For example, since thirteen is commonly considered an unlucky number, some high-rise buildings in the West have no thirteenth floor, and some people try to avoid major undertakings on Friday the thirteenth.

In Chinese society, there are many superstitions. For example, it is said that a high-rise building should not have a fourth floor because the word for the number four in Chinese is homophonic with the word for death, and living on the fourth floor would consequently bring bad luck to the occupants. Travelers avoid staying in room number nine at a hotel because the Chinese word for nine reminds people of death as well. Superstition has other far-reaching impacts on our lives. Some people read their horoscopes before making any decisions. Is this really reliable? Although some people pick lucky days for their wedding, their marriage may still end in divorce. Parents sometimes want to have the fortunes of their newborn children told. They only feel reassured if their newborns wear gold and silver charms on their chests and backs to ensure good fortune. If fortune-tellers are so reliable, can they foresee their own futures? Do they allow this superstitious practice to guide their own destiny?

During the Chinese New Year, it is customary to sweep the floor toward the inside, not the outside, of the house for fear that money will be swept away. It is frequently believed that pregnant women should not recite the *Diamond Sutra* because it is too powerful and may cause miscarriages. However, the *Diamond Sutra* is a sacred scripture. Reciting the sutra will not harm the baby; it is good "prenatal education" for the baby, and the baby's wisdom will grow accordingly. There is another strange custom in Taiwan. When a daughter passes away, she can still participate in an arranged marriage. There are many nice young men who opt to marry a cold memorial tablet instead of a living woman. Superstition is like a rope that tightly binds our hands and feet until we cannot move, and we are often pulled in harmful directions. Superstitious acts are like dark clouds casting heavy shadows, shrouding the radiance of our true nature and impacting our futures in grievous ways. Certainly, none of our individual or communal destinies will blossom with the power of true wisdom if we permit superstition to be our master.

Emotions Control Destiny

Throughout our lives, relationship challenges usually have the most severe impact on us. Many people ruin their futures because of difficult or combative emotional relationships. There are numerous examples of happy families being devastated and ruined by infidelity. If one cannot handle emotions and relationships appropriately, grave misfortune will arise as a natural consequence. Recently, newspapers in Taiwan reported on an affair between Li Wen-pin, the chief of Lu Chou village in Taipei county, and a famous actress. Since the case had to be settled in court, a private emotional dispute became public knowledge. This dispute not only negatively impacted both parties' futures, but also tainted their families' honor.

The sutras say, "One will not be born into the saha world if one does not have strong passions." Some people can resist fame and glory, but they cannot free themselves from the emotional bondage of their family, friends, or lovers. They are mired in conflict and pain. To free ourselves from these shackles, we must use wisdom to open up our minds. We should control our passions and not be controlled by them. In this manner, we also control destiny.

Power Controls Destiny

Power also plays an important role in destiny. Power is often associated with wealth. There is a saying, "The combination of wealth and power is like a tiger getting wings." In other words, a potentially dangerous force can be amplified if we are not careful. A misguided desire for power can corrupt our true nature. Through this selfish priority, too many people have lost themselves, their most valuable possession, in the midst of glory and power. After they have experienced power, they can no longer taste the true flavor of life. Power changes our lives and destinies profoundly. There are at least four ways we can consider the control power exerts over our destinies.

1) Divine Power—Some people choose to seek direction from gods for each choice they encounter, whether it is planning a funeral, a wedding, or some other event. They feel compelled to seek divination before they have peace of mind and can confidently make a decision. They do not care if what they choose has moral value, or if the people they deal with are righteous or not. They believe that as long as the gods will it, they have divine permission, and it can be done. They blindly follow what they believe are the gods' directions, without carefully considering the circumstances themselves and applying their own wisdom. They completely rely upon their gods to make decisions for them and relinquish personal responsibility. In accordance with the saying, "Care not about the mortals, but only about divine consent," these people hand over their lives to their gods with both hands and willingly become their gods' slaves. This is extremely foolish. According to Buddhism, even gods cannot escape the force of karma and the cycle of rebirth; how then can they have the authority to control our destinies?

2) Political Power—Political power controls the life of the general public. If we open a history book, we can easily see the disparity between the lives of those who lived under the rule of a wise and judicious king, and those who lived under a despicable tyrant. Clearly, destinies are shaped and molded by those who form policies and create laws. When we examine today's societies, those who live in open, democratic, and developed countries are much freer and live a better quality of life than those living in totalitarian or autocratic countries, suffering under despotic, tyrannical, and dictatorial

rule. Here in the U.S., we are very fortunate that our destinies are not impacted by the suffering possible under the reign of a tyrannical political figure.

3) Family Power—The kind encouragement of family members can make a child grow strong and ensure that the child travels on the path of success. Family relationships, however, can become excess baggage in a child's cultivation. When I was teaching in Penghu thirty years ago, the niece of a retired mayor gave a very well-received speech on Buddhism. She was an attractive and talented young girl of about seventeen or eighteen years of age. When the audience witnessed her great potential, they encouraged her to study in a Buddhist college to deepen her knowledge about Buddhism. She replied, "No, I cannot. Father said that I should stay home to care for Grandmother." Under the firm instruction of her father, she gave up the opportunity for higher education and for realizing her potential. After twenty years of loving care, her grandmother passed away peacefully. The young, talented girl had become a middle-aged woman, uneducated and bound by family obligations. However, a forty-year-old still has plenty of time to actualize his or her potential and create a productive future. At this point, people once again encouraged her to seize the opportunity to study Buddhism. She replied hesitantly, "Mother and Father said I should care for my aging aunt." Through family pressure, another opportunity slipped away. With time, the aspiration and vitality of youth had dwindled. Although caring for a loved one is both noble and important, this woman's potential was sacrificed for the love and responsibility of family. In our society, many young talents are stifled by family expectations. Real parental love gives a child room to grow and to mold his or her future. Exercising undue control over a child's life can lead to a life full of regrets.

4) The Power of Desire—Desire can exert a frightening hold on our lives and destinies. It often enslaves us and leads us in dangerous directions. At times, when we see others' big mansions and fancy cars, greed dominates our thinking. When these luxuries are beyond one's means, a person driven by desire may resort to swindling others, thievery, and other unlawful means to pursue such luxuries. Desire can tempt us to break the law and become a threat to society; it can also threaten a harmonious destiny. The numerous crime stories in newspapers are human tragedies about people who have submitted to the power of their desires.

Karma Controls Destiny

Finally, the greatest power controlling life is karma. Karma is the product of our acts, including our actions, speech, and thoughts. They are collectively called the "karma of the body, mouth, and mind." Karma determines destiny without exception and can be divided into good and bad. It is said that "All good and evil deeds have their consequences; it is just a matter of time." We will inevitably face the natural and logical results of our acts, whether they are good or bad, when the proper conditions ripen. Although karma controls our lives, we in turn control our karma. For example, we can dilute, or soften, the karma of an improper deed by modifying and correcting our behavior and striving to perform good deeds. If we can improve our conduct, refrain from evil, and seek to benefit others, karma will deliver positive conditions for our lives, and our destinies will be bright and smooth.

Apart from the distinction between good and bad, there are other types of karma. Karma that only affects a single person is called "individual karma," while karma that affects the whole community is called "common karma." For example, people who are born and raised in Taiwan have the same common karma. Although everyone in this saha world has the same common karma, some live in Asia while others live in America. People of many different skin colors exist, including yellow, white, brown, and black. These differences arise because of our own individual karma. In addition to individual and common karma, there are also "determined karma" and "undetermined karma." While some are born into wealth, others are born into poverty. Which family we were born into is beyond our control, because it was decided by our determined karma. Our personal future, however, has yet to be decided and is therefore called undetermined karma. Our future will be determined by our deeds of today. Karma has a powerful and pervasive impact on our lives.

Karma controls destiny, but when does it mature? According to the sutras, it is said that the weightiest common karma will be actualized first. From a time perspective, some karmic effects from our acts of this lifetime will ripen in this life, while other effects will ripen in the next life, or even a few lifetimes from now. This gradual maturation of karma can be compared to planting fruit trees. Some fruit trees bear fruit the year we plant the tree, while others bear fruit only after a few seasons. Regardless of whether we have to wait one, two, or several years, we must diligently sow the seeds if we want to harvest sweet fruits. Similarly, if we want to enjoy the rewards of good karma, we have to plant the proper seeds that encourage its ripening.

How to Change Destiny

Although habits, superstitions, emotions, power, desires, and karma can control our destinies, this does not mean our destinies are fixed. All these controlling factors, from habits to karma, are dictated by our own choices. If we can maintain right mindfulness and be careful in our speech and actions, we can change a destiny of misfortune into a life of brightness and beauty. How, then, can we alter our destinies? What are the methods available?

Views and Perspectives Can Change Destiny

After enlightenment, the Buddha revealed to us the truth of suffering and taught us the way to eradicate suffering by following the Noble Eightfold Path. The most important element of the Noble Eightfold Path is right view. Only when we have the right view do we have a foundation for the other seven elements. Only then will we not go astray. As discussed in the first chapter, right view means having correct understanding and perspective. Correct perspective is critical in advancing one's cultivation. It is also a cornerstone for social progress, economic prosperity, and world peace.

Take the example of Hitler. Although he was an intelligent man, he lacked right view and right understanding. Besides having the ambition to rule the world, he also built many concentration camps and murdered millions of innocent people. His corrupt knowledge and evil views rewrote European history, brought on a great human tragedy, and altered the course of German history, resulting in the split between East and West Germany until recent years. According to Buddhism, it is possible to overcome faults in behavior with relative ease; however, someone with evil views can bring great calamity to society and is much more difficult to reform.

Although there are many factors leading to personal success, a correct perspective is the key ingredient. For example, a parent complains about his lazy son. The son may have no regret at all; instead he may compound the situation with a poor attitude, as if to say, "You said I am lazy. All right, then I'll become a total failure to get back at you." He intentionally avoids any attempt to improve his behavior and willfully becomes a failure. Another person in a similar situation will look within and mend his ways. He works hard to become a success in order to improve others' opinions of him. Two people, in a similar situation with differing views, yield completely different results. Taking it a step further, if we are positive, progressive, and optimistic, no matter what obstacles confront us, we will fight to walk a new path. We will taste the joy of living even in the midst of sorrow. However, if we are passive, regressive, and pessimistic, our outlook will be gray and miserable. To a person with such a depressed attitude, life is mundane and meaningless.

Through these examples, we can see how our views and perspectives directly alter our lives and destinies. A generous person will have an enriched destiny; a miserly person will have an impoverished destiny. If you look at the world with compassion, then life is joyful, the world is beautiful, and the saha world is a pure land. If you look at the world with hatred, then even a pure and wondrous Buddha Land will be transformed into a realm of malice and ugliness. For a harmonious destiny, we have to cultivate the right view and perspective.

Beliefs Can Change Destiny

A life with beliefs is like a voyage with a destination, a journey with direction. Beliefs give purpose to a task and help us to expeditiously work toward our goals without any wasted effort. The power derived from beliefs is like a fine-tuned motor that gives us the energy to proceed and to change our destinies.

We cannot overestimate the importance of beliefs, yet beliefs are not limited to religion. The passion that artists have for their art is a belief. They are willing to expend all their energy toward the creation of a masterpiece. We can open books on the history of human civilization and read how numerous scholars and philosophers have dedicated their lives to their ideals and principles, and thus shaped their destinies in a certain way. The numerous schools of thinkers of the pre-Qin

Dynasty and the Russian Nobel Prize–winning author Alexander Solzhenitsyn are good examples. The legendary General Yue Fei of the Song Dynasty believed in loyalty to his country, and ultimately he sacrificed his life for this belief. His belief in having utmost loyalty to his country changed his life, and he became a model of unwavering allegiance in Chinese history. Even today, General Yue Fei is still worshipped as a folk hero, and his influence can still be felt.

A country's destiny, when not dominated by a crushing and all-powerful dictator, is determined by the beliefs and principles of its citizens. For example, if all Chinese people today can aspire to *The Three Principles of People*[1] (by Dr. Sun Yat-sen) and work together to build their country according to its ideals, it will not be long before China will become prosperous and strong.

Of all beliefs, religious belief is the most powerful. With a strong religious faith, a person can accept the misfortune and duress of life with grace, compassion, and ease. Religious faith can give us courage to endure the most serious setbacks. It opens our hearts and minds to bear the apparent unfairness in life, and it elevates our destinies to a totally different dimension.

Building Good Causal Relationships Can Change Destiny
No person exists or survives independently; we are all essential members of society. Our lives are intertwined with the public at large. Our daily necessities are met through the cooperation of different levels of society. Our knowledge is the result of the patient teaching provided by our teachers at school. Without them, we would remain ignorant. Even when we finally become working members of society, we still need the help of our colleagues and the mentoring of our superiors before we can reach our potential and make a substantial contribution. If we want to be effective and successful, we need to develop

---

1. This book discusses the democratic ideology of the founder of modern China.

and maintain friendly relationships with others. The sutras say, "Before learning the Buddhist teachings, first work to establish good causal relationships with others." In Buddhism, the phrase "building good causal relationships" means constructing amiable and mutually beneficial social connections with others.

If we want to build a multitude of good causal relationships with others, we should be friendly and helpful. With the established relationships, we will be rewarded with great convenience throughout our lives. Helping others is really helping ourselves. When we give to others, we are actually giving to ourselves. Since we all are one, we should not view people in terms of "us versus them"; it is only through helping others that we can experience personal development and fulfillment. Thus, bodhisattvas look at helping sentient beings as a means of cultivation. It is through building Dharma relationships with all sentient beings that bodhisattvas reach Buddhahood. Building good causal relationships not only changes our destiny; it is also an important gateway for entering into the Buddhist teachings. In our daily lives, a friendly smile, a word of encouragement, a helping hand, and sincere concern can all bring great joy to others and help to strengthen friendly relations. Building good causal relations broadens our horizons and paves the way for a good destiny. With such benefits, why should we not direct our energy and effort this way?

Upholding the Precepts Can Change Destiny

In addition to views, beliefs, and building good causal relationships, upholding the precepts can also change our destinies. Refraining from killing prolongs a short lifespan. Refraining from stealing transforms poverty into wealth. Refraining from sexual misconduct builds family harmony. Refraining from lying results in a good reputation. Refraining from intoxicants protects our health and our mental faculties. Without question, upholding the precepts can change a life of misery into a happy and healthy one.

In the sutras, there is a story of how the act of protecting life altered a destiny. Once, there was a merchant who was at the market shopping. There he saw a little caged turtle staring at him with teary eyes. At that very moment, compassion arose in his heart, and he decided to buy the turtle. He promptly took the turtle to a pond and set him free. A while later, when the merchant was out on business, he was robbed by bandits as he traveled on a mountain road. The bandits took all his money and pushed him into a lake. Just as he was about to drown, he felt support under his feet. With the help of this support, he was able to make it safely to shore. Afterwards, he realized that the little turtle that he had saved earlier, together with his companions, had supported him to repay him for extending the turtle's life. Thus, if we can refrain from killing and protect the lives of all sentient beings, our blessings will definitely grow and our destinies will be rich with kind assistance and convenience.

Everyone has a destiny. It is controlled by many factors. To break loose of these controls and build our own lives, we must have the right view and a strong faith, build a multitude of good causal relations, and uphold the precepts. Through our own efforts, we are not under the control of destiny; we can freely master it.

THE BUDDHIST VIEW ON LIFE AND DESTINY

Destiny is such a wondrous mystery. What do the Buddhist teachings reveal on this subject? I address four main points below.

Buddhism Believes Destiny Is Not Fixed;
Instead, It Is Alterable

Although Buddhism believes in the existence of destiny, it differs from the pre-determinism of some other religions. In Buddhism, destiny is not handed to us in a preset, fixed package. It is much more dynamic and empowering than this. Buddhism teaches that all existence arises out of causes and conditions, and that existence is empty and without a separate independent self or nature. Thus, destiny is also dependent on causes and conditions, and is without an independent self or nature. We can intentionally and compassionately plant good seeds to alter our misfortunes and redirect our destinies. There is a famous tale of a young sramanera (novice monk) that illustrates this point well.

Once there was an old arhat master. In his samadhi, he saw that one of his favorite young disciples had only seven more days to live. He thought to himself, "Why does this good child only have seven more days to live? This is most unfortunate! I cannot tell him this. How can he withstand such trauma?"

Early the next day, the master contained his sadness and asked the sramanera to come before him, "My good child, you have not seen your parents for a long time. Go home and pay them a visit."

The sramanera, not knowing what was going to happen, felt that his master was acting in an odd manner. Nevertheless, he packed up, happily said goodbye to his master, and went on his way. Seven days went by, and the sramanera had not returned. Though the arhat was free from all worldly defilements, he was concerned about the welfare of his sramanera. He was still mourning the fact that he would never see his young disciple again when the sramanera suddenly and unexpectedly returned. The arhat was shocked! He held the sramanera's hand, looked him over carefully, and asked, "How did you manage to return safely? What have you done in the last few days?"

Puzzled, the sramanera shook his head and replied, "Nothing."

The arhat continued to question him, "Think carefully. Did you see anything? Do anything?"

"Oh, yes, there was one thing," the sramanera replied

earnestly. "On my way home, I passed by a pond and saw a colony of ants drowning. So I picked up a leaf and ferried them all to shore."

After the arhat heard this tale of kindness, he entered a state of meditation to see the destiny of the young sramanera. He saw that not only was the disciple not going to die young, but his life had been extended to a hundred years. Through a single act of compassion, he had saved the ants' lives and changed his own destiny.

In addition to compassion, merit can also change a life from disastrous to wondrous. Some people feel that because of their heinous crimes they are beyond help, that there is no way they can transform themselves and turn their lives around. This is not the case at all. Buddhism teaches that even the gravest karma can be lessened. Negative karmic effects can be compared to a handful of salt put into a glass of water. The water will be too salty to drink. However, if the salt is poured into a large basin or a tank of water, it will not be salty at all. The salt of wrongdoing, no matter how strong, can be diluted by the plentiful water of good merits, even to the point of making the water palatable. Similarly, in a neglected field where weeds have grown among the rice seedlings, if we work diligently to eradicate the weeds, the rice seedlings will have a chance to grow. Once the rice seedlings of merit are tall and strong, even if there are a few weeds here and there, the harvest will still be bountiful. Even the karma of the most evil transgressions can be modified by the strength of virtue and merit.

One of the ten great vows of the Samantabhadra Bodhisattva is to help all beings repent of their evil deeds. Repentance is another way to alter our destiny. It will eradicate the evil karma, allowing space for our wisdom and blessings to grow. Dirty laundry can be cleansed with pure water. A filthy body can be washed clean by bathing. A sinful mind can be sanctified with the Dharma water of sincere repentance, returning it to its original state. There is a saying, "Repent of your old sins according to your circumstances and conditions, and do not commit new ones." If we can be sincere and steadfast in our repentance, we can remove the filth of our defilements and let our original, pure nature show through. Repentance services are very important religious ceremonies in the Buddhist liturgy. Many venerables of the past have set examples for us on how to conduct repentance services. Examples include the Compassion Water Repentance Service, Emperor Wu's Repentance Service, and the Three Modes of Repentance of the Tian Tai School.

Destiny is not static and unalterable. It can be affected by compassion, merit, and repentance. The accumulation of merits and virtues can enable a new life to emerge out of the most hopeless situation. However, if a person with a smooth and peaceful destiny does not know how to honor and treasure his or her good fortune, he or she will confront hardship. This idea reinforces the saying, "When you live in safety, watch out for disaster." We need to practice gracious awareness and offer heartfelt appreciation for the joy in our lives.

Buddhism Regards the Past as Important but Places More Emphasis on the Present and Future

In Buddhism, the Law of Cause and Effect spans our past, present, and future lives. Although Buddhism believes that our fate is determined by causes from the past, it places more emphasis on what can be done in the present to build a better future. The past cannot be changed, and dwelling on it does not serve a purpose. However, we have ultimate freedom and power to design our future. If we can navigate the present properly, a bright destiny awaits us. Thus, according to Buddhism, one should not wallow in past regrets but should actively pursue an infinitely hopeful and joyous future.

How do we change a life of misfortune into a beautiful future?

To do so, we have to improve our character; transform our heart; change our words, thoughts and actions; and make amends for our wrongdoings. There is a common saying, "It is easier to move mountains than to change one's character." Redirecting our focus and our actions is not quick or simple, but it is essential for cultivating a brilliant future. Undertaking a personal transformation requires dedicated spiritual development.

If we can change our entrenched bad habits, soften our raging tempers, and open ourselves up to others, our destinies will improve correspondingly. In this modern age of organ transplants, someone with heart disease can receive a new heart that will enable him or her to lead a vibrant life. When our physical heart is damaged, we need to consult a physician. When our spiritual heart is defective, we need to change it into a heart of virtue, kindness, and righteousness before we can have a healthy life.

Character modification is the prescription for changing our destinies; repentance and making amends are medicine for building new futures. Many headaches and sorrows arise because we do not know how to "turn ourselves around." Unfortunately, we are quite skilled at blindly pushing forward, unknowingly forcing ourselves into a small corner and a limited life. If we can always allow some room to maneuver and some space to retreat and ponder, we will find that the world is much bigger, with more potential, than we ever imagined.

Buddhism Does Not Encourage People to Resign Themselves to Fate, but Teaches People to Build Their Own Destiny

In the midst of misfortune, some people think that their ill fortune is divinely assigned and that it is useless to struggle against this godly design. In relinquishing their individual responsibility, they became glum, frustrated, and passive. They put their precious future into the hands of their imagined gods and willingly become enslaved. Buddhism, however, believes that destiny is within our control. Nobody, not even gods, can dictate our destinies. We are our own masters; we are the architects of our own future. The Buddha is a good example that we can emulate.

Before achieving Buddhahood, the Buddha was a prince, enjoying unparalleled worldly pleasure and respect. He was not satisfied, however, with the palace lifestyle and refused to be a mediocre person trapped in the assumptions and expectations of his family lineage. He relinquished his fame, wealth, family, and loved ones. He chose to seek the path of truth on his own, and in doing so he built a boundless life for himself. The Buddha's enlightenment also opened a new door for all sentient beings seeking happy and fulfilling futures for themselves.

Human destiny is not fixed and unchangeable. Heaven cannot turn us into saints, nor can it make us become lowly and submissive. It is said that "There is no natural Sakyamuni Buddha." All saints and sages accomplished their merits of their own accord and with great effort. If we work diligently, the life of wisdom is ours to know and experience.

Buddhism Not Only Encourages Us to Be Content but Also Hopes that We Can Improve the Future

Confucius once said, "It was only when I was fifty that I knew what heaven had planned." If a sage like Confucius was able to see the truth of the universe only after he had reached mature middle age, we can understand that it is not an easy task to accept life as it is. Buddhism takes this a step further and teaches us that in addition to accepting life with grace, we must also take steps to improve our future.

The Buddha was a great religious teacher with concern and compassion for all beings. He was also a courageous and moral revolutionary. During his time, the Buddha openly protested against the ills of the caste system and taught us how to eradicate all of our spiritual defilements. Thus the Buddha's revolution is achieved not by hurting others but by self-reflection and the development of character. It is not aimed externally but instead internally, through recognizing and eliminating our desires. It is only when we work courageously to transform ourselves that we can truly have a bright future.

Most of us fall into the trap of criticizing others' shortcomings and excusing our own. The Buddha taught the Dharma for several decades, giving us numerous methods to wash away the defilements of our hearts and minds in order to help us return them to their clear, pure, original state—our true nature. The process of cultivation is none other than the cleansing of our hearts and the purification of our lives. When the sky is clear, the moon will naturally shine through. Similarly, when we are purified, we will join the ranks of Buddhahood in the ultimate emptiness. It is my greatest hope that we can all build brilliant destinies for ourselves with this wisdom.

GLOSSARY

Alaya-vijnana: Literally "storehouse of consciousness." Regarded in the Yogacara or Mind-Only school of the Mahayana tradition as the repository of the essential consciousness of everything that exists. It contains the karmic seeds of individual lives, which in turn give rise to new mental activity. Sometimes also referred to as *alaya consciousness.*

Amitabha Buddha: The Buddha of the Western Pure Land, also known as the Buddha of Infinite Light. Amitabha Buddha is described as vowing to purify a realm for those who desire to seek rebirth there by earnestly reciting his name. Sometimes referred to as Amita Buddha or Amitayus Buddha (the Buddha of Infinite Life).

Arhat: The ideal of the Theravadan Buddhist tradition. The *arhat* is one who has attained enlightenment through personal devotion and adherence to the Buddha's teachings. *Arhats* are no longer subject to the cycle of birth and death.

Asura: A malevolent spirit who was once a sentient being whose arrogant thoughts, words, and actions dominated his living and directed the karma or momentum of his intentional life choices toward this rebirth. The *asura* is one of the Eight Divisions of Deities. Although known for his contentious nature, the *asura* is sometimes relied upon as a protector of Buddhism.

Bhagavat: Also spelled "Bhagava." One of the ten epithets of a Buddha. Literally, it means "fortunate, prosperous, happy, divine, adorable, and venerable." Because the Buddha has already eliminated all affliction and unwholesomeness, and attained enlightenment, he is the most venerable one.

Bodhi: "Awakened" or "enlightened." In the state of *bodhi*, one is awakened to one's own Buddha Nature, thus eliminating all afflictions and delusions. Gaining a *bodhi*-mind can be understood as the attainment of *prajna*-wisdom.

Bodhicitta: The *bodhi* or "awakened" mind, or mind seeking to achieve enlightenment. In the Mahayana tradition it refers to the mind of an altruistic practitioner who has vowed to attain enlightenment to save all sentient beings.

Bodhisattva: An enlightened being. *Bodhi* means "enlightened" and *sattva* refers to "sentient beings." Therefore, the term *bodhisattva* refers to a being that has attained enlightenment through practicing all six *paramitas*. Bodhisattvas vow to remain in the world, postponing their own full enlightenment in entering nirvana, in order to liberate all beings. The *bodhisattva* ideal is the main defining feature of Mahayana Buddhism.

Buddha: Literally "The awakened one." Used as a generic term to refer to one who has achieved enlightenment and attained complete liberation from the cycle of existence (see *samsara*). More commonly used to refer to the Sakyamuni Buddha, the historical founder of Buddhism (581–501 BCE). He was born the prince of Kapilavastu as the son of King Suddhodana. At the age of twenty-nine he left the royal palace and his family to search for the meaning of existence. Six years later, he attained enlightenment under the Bodhi tree. He then spent the next forty-five years expounding his teachings, which include the Four Noble Truths, the Noble Eightfold Path, the Law of Cause and Effect, and the Law of Dependent Origination. At the age of eighty, he entered the state of *parinirvana*.

Buddha Nature: The true nature or inherent potential for achieving Buddhahood that exists in all beings.

Chan: A school of Buddhism that emphasizes enlightenment through deep contemplation, meditation, and internal cultivation. Practicing Chan Buddhism does not rely upon intellectual reasoning, analysis of doctrine, or academic studies, but upon a profound inner concentration that can reveal and illuminate one's true nature. (Synonym: Zen.)

Deva: Literally "Shining One." Term for celestial beings that live in the realm of the heavens but are still subject to the cycle of rebirth.

Devadatta: Cousin of the Sakyamuni Buddha who became a highly respected member of the *sangha*. Eight years before the death of the Buddha, he tried unsuccessfully to murder the Buddha and place himself as the head of the community. Brought about schism in the Buddhist Order.

Dharma: Literally "law." Usually refers to the teachings of the Buddha. When capitalized, it means: 1) the ultimate truth, and 2) the teachings of the Buddha. When the Dharma is applied or practiced in life it is referred to as: 3) righteousness or virtues. When it appears with a lowercase "d," it means: 4) anything that can be thought of, experienced, or named; close in meaning to "phenomena."

Dharmadatu: As a space, it can have many interchangeable meanings, including realms of mind, cosmos, reality or truth. As a notion, it refers to the underlying nature of all phenomena.

Dhyana: Meditation or concentration. It refers to the practice of relying on meditative absorption to reach a state of enlightenment. The Chinese term for this is *Chan* and the Japanese is "Zen."

Five Aggregates: Indicating form, feeling, perception, mental formation, and consciousness, which together and *interdependently* constitute what we commonly regard as an "individual personality." Also referred to as the "five *skandhas*."

Five Precepts: Guiding principles in Buddhism that teach proper conduct. They include abstaining from: 1) killing, 2) stealing, 3) sexual misconduct, 4) lying, and 5) ingesting intoxicating substances.

Four Noble Truths: A fundamental Buddhist teaching about the nature and existence of suffering: 1) the truth of suffering, 2) the truth of the cause of suffering, 3) the truth of cessation of suffering, and 4) the path leading to the cessation of suffering.

Karma: Defined as "work, action, or deeds" and related to the Law of Cause and Effect. All mental, verbal and physical deeds that are governed by *intention*, whether good or bad, produce effects. The effects may be experienced instantly, or they may accumulate and not come to fruition for many years or even many lifetimes.

Mahayana: Literally means "The Great Vehicle," referring to one of the two main traditions of Buddhism, the other being Theravada. Mahayana Buddhism stresses that helping all sentient beings attain enlightenment is more important than just self-liberation.

Nirvana: Literally "extinction," but also can mean "calmed, quieted, tamed, or ceasing." In Buddhism, it refers to the absolute extinction of individual existence, or of all afflictions and desires; it is the state of liberation, beyond birth and death. It is also the final spiritual goal in all branches of Buddhism.

Noble Eightfold Path: Eight right ways leading to the cessation of suffering according to the Four Noble Truths taught by the Buddha. They are: 1) right view, 2) right thought, 3) right speech, 4) right action, 5) right livelihood, 6) right effort, 7) right mindfulness, and 8) right concentration.

Prajna: Literally "consciousness" or "wisdom." As the highest form of wisdom, *prajna* is the wisdom of insight into "emptiness," which is the true nature of all phenomena. The realization of *prajna* also implies the attainment of enlightenment and is in this sense one of the six *paramitas* or "perfections" of the *bodhisattva* path. Sometimes referred to by the compound term *prajna-wisdom*.

Pratyeka-buddha: Literally "solitary awakened one." Refers to a practitioner seeking enlightenment through the contemplation of the Law of Cause and Condition not to teach others, but for his or her own liberation. In the Mahayana tradition, the *pratyeka-buddha* is placed between the *arhats* and the Buddhas who have achieved full enlightenment.

Precepts: Generally speaking, the rules of conduct for all Buddhists. There are separate precepts for monastics and for lay practitioners. However, in the Mahayana tradition there is also a special category referred to as the "Bodhisattva Precepts," followed by all practitioners.

Pure Land: Pure Land practice can be traced back to India and the teachings of the Buddha. It remains the most popular worldwide of all the 84,000 different Buddhist paths to supreme enlightenment. The Pure Land practitioner seeks rebirth in the Pure Land of Amitabha Buddha first through cultivating the *bodhicitta*, or the desire for enlightenment; second, through the practice of reciting the name of Amitabha Buddha with sincerity and deep devotion, as well as cultivating one's life through the three trainings of precepts, concentration, and *prajna*. Together, they enable one to more rapidly purify the mind and liberate oneself from all delusions. Although one is not free from all wants and fears in the Pure Land, they no longer bind one. The Pure Land can also be found in this world by the devout practitioner.

Saha: The term is often used to describe the galaxy in which we live—the galaxy of suffering and dissatisfaction. It is said to be composed of one billion worlds. Saha literally means "endurance." It is a way to describe human beings in this world who are most willing to endure perpetual suffering arising from the three poisons of greed, anger, and delusion, as well as all kinds of insatiable desires.

Samadhi: The highest state of mind achieved through meditation, chanting, reciting the Buddha's name, or other practices, in which the mind has reached ultimate concentration and is not subject to thoughts and distractions. The highest state of *samadhi* is the *bodhi* or enlightened mind.

Samsara: The endless cycle of birth and death.

Sangha: Refers specifically to the community of monastics or more generally to the Buddhist community that includes both monastics and laypersons. The *sangha* is considered one of the Triple Gems in Buddhism.

Six Dusts: Indicating the six objects reflected by the six "roots" (sense-organs), which then produce the six types of consciousness.

Six Paramitas: Also known as the "six perfections" that *bodhisattvas* attain in the course of their development. *Paramita* in Sanskrit literally means "gone to the other shore," which can also imply reaching transcendental perfection or complete attainment. The six *paramitas* or perfections are: 1) charity, 2) moral discipline, 3) patience, 4) diligence, 5) meditation, and 6) *prajna*.

Six Realms of Existence: Indicating the realms of heaven, *asura*, human, animal, hungry ghost, and hell.

Sramanera: A male novice, often a young person, who has vowed to practice the ten precepts but is not yet a fully ordained monk. A *sramanika* is a female novice.

Sravaka: Literally "hearer." *Sravakas* liberate themselves from the cycle of rebirth by "hearing" the Buddha's teachings and attaining *arhatship*, the ideal in Theravadan Buddhist practice. In contrast to the *bodhisattva* of the Mahayana tradition, the *sravaka*, upon fulfilling the *arhat* ideal, chooses not to remain in the cycle of rebirth to benefit all sentient beings and instead enters nirvana.

Sunyata: Literally "emptiness" or "void." A central concept in Buddhism, which asserts that everything existing in the world is due to dependent origination and has no permanent self or substance. Its meaning can be applied to two groups: 1) emptiness of living beings, which means that human beings or other living beings have no unchanging, substantial self; or 2) emptiness of *dharmas*, which means that the existence of all phenomena is due to causes and conditions. Unlike nihilism, this concept does not imply that nothing exists, rather it stresses that all existence is without independent substance or absolute essence.

Sutra: Literally "threaded together." Refers to the scriptures taught directly by the Buddha and recorded by his disciples for all to follow in their practice. The direct attribution of the teachings to the Buddha is implied in the opening line of each sutra, "Thus have I heard."

Ten Virtuous Practices: Buddhist teachings that instruct practitioners to: 1) protect and nurture life, 2) abstain from stealing, 3) abstain from sexual misconduct, 4) speak truthfully, 5) foster good relationships, 6) speak gently and use encouraging words, 7) speak sincerely, 8) practice generosity, 9) practice patience and tolerance, and 10) uphold the right view.

Theravada: Literally "teaching of the elders of the order" in Pali. One of the eighteen schools in the Period of Sectarian Buddhism. Unlike the *bodhisattva* ideal in Mahayana tradition, its emphasis is on the liberation of the individual. In the third century BCE, it was transmitted to Sri Lanka from India. Today it is popular in many areas of Southeast Asia.

Twelve Links of Conditioned Arising: The twelve links in the chain of existence or the twelve conditions that keep us in the wheel of rebirth. The twelve conditions are: 1) ignorance, 2) activity, conception, and disposition, 3) consciousness, 4) name and form, 5) the six sense organs, i.e., eyes, ears, nose, tongue, body, and mind, 6) contact, 7) sensation or feelings, 8) thirst, desire, and craving, 9) grasping or clinging, 10) being or existing, 11) birth, and 12) old age and death.

Vinaya: Body of precise precepts, or rules, that monks and nuns are required to follow.

Yama: Yama is the ruler of the hell realms who rewards beings with the painful results of their karmic choices. Hell, like all other realms of the *saha* world, is subject to impermanence. When people learn how the momentum of their choices has put them in hell, they can discern how to break their habitual tendencies and release themselves from hell.